How Does Cell Phone Use Impact Teenagers?

Patricia D. Netzley

INCONTROVERSY

ReferencePoint
Press®

San Diego, CA

© 2013 ReferencePoint Press, Inc.
Printed in the United States

For more information, contact:
ReferencePoint Press, Inc.
PO Box 27779
San Diego, CA 92198
www.ReferencePointPress.com

LIBRARY OF CONGRESS CATALOGING-IN-PUBLICATION DATA

Netzley, Patricia D.
    How does cell phone use impact teenagers? / by Patricia D. Netzley.
        p. cm. -- (In controversy series)
    Includes bibliographical references and index.
    ISBN 978-1-60152-446-1 (hardback) -- ISBN 1-60152-446-3 (hardback)
1. Cell phones--Social aspects--Juvenile literature. 2. Teenagers--Social life and culture--Juvenile literature. I. Title.
    HE9713.N489   2013
    303.48'33--dc23
                                                                            2012020756

Contents

Foreword

In 2008, as the US economy and economies worldwide were falling into the worst recession since the Great Depression, most Americans had difficulty comprehending the complexity, magnitude, and scope of what was happening. As is often the case with a complex, controversial issue such as this historic global economic recession, looking at the problem as a whole can be overwhelming and often does not lead to understanding. One way to better comprehend such a large issue or event is to break it into smaller parts. The intricacies of global economic recession may be difficult to understand, but one can gain insight by instead beginning with an individual contributing factor, such as the real estate market. When examined through a narrower lens, complex issues become clearer and easier to evaluate.

This is the idea behind ReferencePoint Press's *In Controversy* series. The series examines the complex, controversial issues of the day by breaking them into smaller pieces. Rather than looking at the stem cell research debate as a whole, a title would examine an important aspect of the debate such as *Is Stem Cell Research Necessary?* or *Is Embryonic Stem Cell Research Ethical?* By studying the central issues of the debate individually, researchers gain a more solid and focused understanding of the topic as a whole.

Each book in the series provides a clear, insightful discussion of the issues, integrating facts and a variety of contrasting opinions for a solid, balanced perspective. Personal accounts and direct quotes from academic and professional experts, advocacy groups, politicians, and others enhance the narrative. Sidebars add depth to the discussion by expanding on important ideas and events. For quick reference, a list of key facts concludes every chapter. Source notes, an annotated organizations list, bibliography, and index provide student researchers with additional tools for papers and class discussion.

The *In Controversy* series also challenges students to think critically about issues, to improve their problem-solving skills, and to sharpen their ability to form educated opinions. As President Barack Obama stated in a March 2009 speech, success in the twenty-first century will not be measurable merely by students' ability to "fill in a bubble on a test but whether they possess 21st century skills like problem-solving and critical thinking and entrepreneurship and creativity." Those who possess these skills will have a strong foundation for whatever lies ahead.

No one can know for certain what sort of world awaits today's students. What we can assume, however, is that those who are inquisitive about a wide range of issues; open-minded to divergent views; aware of bias and opinion; and able to reason, reflect, and reconsider will be best prepared for the future. As the international development organization Oxfam notes, "Today's young people will grow up to be the citizens of the future: but what that future holds for them is uncertain. We can be quite confident, however, that they will be faced with decisions about a wide range of issues on which people have differing, contradictory views. If they are to develop as global citizens all young people should have the opportunity to engage with these controversial issues."

In Controversy helps today's students better prepare for tomorrow. An understanding of the complex issues that drive our world and the ability to think critically about them are essential components of contributing, competing, and succeeding in the twenty-first century.

Heavy Usage

At around 9:15 p.m. on March 23, 2012, sixteen-year-old Haylie Samuelson, a junior in high school, was driving on a highway near Hinckley, Minnesota, when her car veered off the road, hit the edge of a driveway, and flipped over several times. Samuelson, who was not wearing a seat belt, was thrown from the car and killed. Her passenger, a teen who was wearing a seat belt, survived.

Many people believe Samuelson would still be alive if she had buckled up when she got behind the wheel. But others also blame the teen's death on her cell phone, because Samuelson lost control of her car while using it to send a text message to a friend. One of her classmates, Theo Hedtke, later told a reporter that the circumstances of Samuelson's accident had served as a warning to other teens at her school. "A lot of people said they were going to wear their seat belts," he explained, "and they are going to keep their phone in their purse or pocket."[1]

However, this resolve might be hard to keep given how heavily most teens use their cell phones. According to the Pew Research Center, as of December 2011, 80 percent of young people ages fourteen to seventeen and 66 percent of those ages twelve and thirteen use cell phones regularly, and other studies indicate that over 50 percent of teens send text messages (an activity also known as texting) every day, with more than half of them sending at least 50 text messages a day. A Nielsen survey conducted in the second half of 2010 found that teens between the ages of thirteen and seventeen sent and received 3,339 text messages on their cell phones each month, whereas adults ages forty-five to fifty-four sent and received only 323 text messages a month. In fact, the Pew Research Center says, "Text messaging has become the primary way that teens reach their friends, surpassing face-to-face contact, email, instant messaging and voice calling as the go-to daily communication tool."[2]

Internet Access

Teens who have the most sophisticated cell phones can use them to go online in addition to sending and receiving text messages. This enables them to visit websites, update blogs, download and listen to music, send e-mails and instant messages, and play web-based games no matter where they are. With all of these features within easy reach, many teens are tempted to use their phones when it is unwise to do so. In fact, studies have confirmed that teens have a greater tendency than adults to use their cell phones at inappropriate times. For example, whereas less than one-fourth of all drivers admit to having sent text messages while behind the wheel, nearly half of drivers under the age of eighteen say they engage in this behavior. In addition, nearly 60 percent of teens who attend a school that bans cell phone use during class claim to have sent and received text messages in class despite the ban.

At the teen website Teen Ink, a teen from Moraga, California, writing under the screen name jnazeri12, complains about the excessive use of cell phones among teens, saying: "Most of the time you witness your classmates heads down staring at the lit up screen [of their phones while in class] and their fingers moving fifty miles an hour trying to finish off the text they need so badly to send to their best friend before they arrive at their next class. Devices such as cell phones and computers have caused teenagers to become too reliant on technology."[3]

Hypertexting

Teens have a greater tendency than adults not only to text but to hypertext. Psychologists use this term to refer to the sending of more than 120 text messages a day, which they consider excessive enough to be a matter of concern. According to a 2010 study

> "Text messaging has become the primary way that teens reach their friends, surpassing face-to-face contact, email, instant messaging and voice calling as the go-to daily communication tool."[2]
>
> — Pew Research Center, a nonprofit organization that conducts and analyzes the results of public opinion polls and demographic studies.

Today's teens rely on cell phones for communication, information, entertainment, and more. While they may be more technologically sophisticated than teens of earlier generations, some experts caution that they have become overly dependent on their cell phones.

by the American Public Health Association, teens who hypertext have a much greater tendency to abuse drugs or alcohol, to get into fights, and to be sexually promiscuous. Other studies indicate that teens who send a lot of texts are more likely to engage in sexting, the practice of texting sexually explicit photos or videos or sexually charged messages.

Excessive texting can also lead to health problems. Among the most common is text message injury (TMI), which results in injury to the thumb after repetitive text messaging. TMI can also affect the hand and wrist, and sufferers sometimes experience pain in the arm, shoulder, and neck as well. In addition, people who text while walking can injure themselves by tripping and falling or by accidentally running into things, and excessive texting can disrupt sleep. Some health experts also believe that the radiation emitted by the phones can cause tumors or infertility among those who use them excessively—especially teens, because their brains and bodies are still developing. Others reject this idea, arguing that cell phones are no more harmful than other electronic devices.

Benefits

Even experts who warn against excessive cell phone use acknowledge that phones provide many benefits to society. They allow people to stay connected to friends and family, for example, and provide a way to report crimes and emergencies in remote places where a landline might not be easily accessible. They also make it easier for teens to call their parents for a ride home, or to report a change in plans, or to ask for help, advice, or permission to do something.

Some experts believe that using a cell phone has psychological benefits for the user as well. For example, language expert David Crystal says that texting provides "reserved, introverted, or nervous pupils" with an increase in "their expressive confidence."[4] In his book *Txtng: The Gr8 Db8* he quotes an expert in social communication, Kate Fox, as saying that in her studies of teens who text, "texting can help them to overcome their awkwardness and develop their social and communication skills; they communicate with more people, and communicate more frequently, than they did before having access to mobile texting."[5]

Crystal complains that "texting has been blamed for all kinds of evils that it could not possibly have been responsible for."[6] Other experts counter that while cell phone use might be fine in moderation, the kind of heavy usage seen among teens does cause serious problems. Still others say that while these problems do exist, their degree of severity has been exaggerated by the media. Indeed, research on cell phone–related

"Texting has been blamed for all kinds of evils that it could not possibly have been responsible for."[6]

— Language and texting expert David Crystal.

problems often yields widely varying results; for example, in some surveys less than 5 percent of teens said they had engaged in sexting, while in others 39 percent of teens admitted to sexting. Such disparities make it difficult for people to determine exactly how and to what degree cell phone use is affecting society.

Facts

- Over 95 percent of sixteen- to seventeen-year-olds in Japan own their own cell phones.

- According to the Pew Research Center, 90 percent of parents with children under the age of 18 living at home have a cell phone, whereas only 72 percent of adults without such children have one.

CHAPTER ONE

What Are the Origins of the Teen Cell Phone Use Controversy?

In a March 2012 post on a financial advice website, Sarah Gilbert reports that a friend's twelve-year-old daughter, "Sophie," incurred a huge cell phone bill because of excessive texting. "Her parents didn't have any idea this was going on," Gilbert says. "They'd set the bill to autopay a fixed amount each month."[7] When the overage remained unpaid, the company suspended use of the phone, and Sophie's father discovered that he owed several hundred dollars. He had to use some of the family's savings to pay the debt.

Similarly, in 2010, after his cell phone company mistakenly put him on a plan that did not include unlimited text messaging, thirteen-year-old Matthew Penzo ran up a $1,055 bill for sending and receiving roughly four thousand text messages. Until his father, Len Penzo, received the 141-page bill, he had no idea that his son—who had had the cell phone only for a few months—was texting so heavily. This was also the case with the parents of seventeen-year-old Sofia Rubenstein of Washington, DC, whose bill was $1,100 for just one month of cell phone use. Rubenstein's cell phone plan allowed her only 100 free text messages a month, but she used 6,807. When she found out about the "incredible" number of messages she had sent and what the cost would be, she says, "I just thought, oh my God, my life is *over*."[8] Her parents made her work in their retail store to pay off the bill.

Bill Shock

For many parents, getting a large bill is the first sign that their teens might have a problem with excessive cell phone use. "It just hit us like a rock, like you're stepping into a bus,"[9] says Gregg Christoffersen, whose thirteen-year-old daughter racked up nearly $5,000 in cell phone charges in just one month. Until he received the bill, Christoffersen had no idea that the teenager had been sending and receiving hundreds of text messages a day while at school. Ted Estarija of Hayward, California, had a similar reaction after receiving a $21,917 bill because his thirteen-year-old son used his cell phone excessively in order to watch videos, play games, and listen to music. "I was completely caught off guard,"[10] Estarija says. Unemployed at the time and unable to pay the bill, he contacted reporters to call attention to his plight, and the cell phone company eventually waived the charges.

A Recent Problem

According to the Federal Communications Commission, at least 30 million Americans, or one out of every six cell phone users, have been shocked by an unexpectedly large cell phone bill. But in the early years of cell phone use, teens were rarely the cause of such overages because few teens had access to a cell phone. Moreover, the devices could be used only to make phone calls, so texting was not an issue.

The first handheld mobile cellular phone appeared in the 1970s. Back then, cell phones were much larger and heavier than today's models. For example, the device that made the world's first cell phone call in 1973, a Motorola DynaTAC, weighed two pounds. Not until the 1990s did cell phones begin to have the

National Texting Championship

In October 2011 sixteen-year-old Austin Wierschke from Rhinelander, Wisconsin, won fifty thousand dollars in the fifth annual LG US National Texting Championship, sponsored by LG Electronics, thereby earning the title of fastest texter in the United States as well as the right to compete in the 2012 LG Mobile World Cup. To prepare for the national event, Wierschke doubled his usual texting habit of six hundred words a day to twelve hundred words a day. However, the competition involved more than just simple texting. There were several rounds to eliminate competitors. One round, for example, involved typing while blindfolded. Others involved typing phrases backward, typing words from memory, typing words made from scrambled letters, or typing while being distracted by cheerleaders. In the last round, Wierschke had to compete against the reigning 2010 champion, fourteen-year-old Brianna Hendrickson. She also appears in the 2011 documentary *Thumbs*, produced by MTV and directed by Academy Award–winning director Bill Couturié, which follows six teens between the ages of thirteen and sixteen who were among the final thirty-two competitors in the 2010 National Texting Championship. That year, some of the teens were able to type one hundred words per minute on the LG phones used in the competition.

capabilities that today's users associate with the device. For example, the first text message, then called an SMS (for "short message service") was sent in 1992, and in 1993 Motorola Inc. introduced a phone that weighed much less than others, the 3-ounce StarTAC (85g), which was also the first clamshell phone (a phone that opens and closes like a clamshell). The first downloaded content—a ringtone—became available in 1998, and around this same time the first consumer smartphones appeared, among them the BlackBerry in 1999. Smartphones are devices that act not only as mobile phones but personal computers; early versions had limited features, but today's models may include, in addition to full Internet access, MP3 players, cameras, and a GPS (global positioning system, which helps people find their way from one location to another).

Fashion Accessories

As technology improved, the desire to have a cell phone dramatically increased among teens. However, some experts believe that one particular phone is largely responsible for an explosion of teen cell phone users in the early 2000s: the RAZR cell phone. At the time this phone was introduced, only one in five teens had a cell phone, but shortly after RAZR's introduction the number of teen users began to climb.

The main reason for this phone's popularity among teens was its appearance. While other phones on the market at that time were designed to appeal to businesspeople, the RAZR was designed as a fashion accessory. Manufactured by Motorola Inc. from late 2004 until July 2007 (at which point it was replaced by the less popular RAZR 2), the RAZR came in teen-appealing colors, including hot pink, and it had a sleek clamshell design. In addition, marketing campaigns presented it as something that glamorous people would have. For example, in 2005 it was offered free to celebrities attending the Academy Awards.

By July 2006, over 50 million RAZR phones had been sold, and by 2008 over 130 million had been sold. (Motorola's current version of the phone is the Droid RAZR.) Meanwhile, other companies launched competing phones into the marketplace, the most notable being the Nokia N95 in 2007, the first smartphone for ordinary consumers that included a GPS, and the Apple iPhone, also introduced in 2007, the first smartphone to feature a touch-sensitive display instead of keys. With so many choices and advanced features to attract teens, the number of kids in the United States who have a cell phone rose to over 75 percent in 2010, and today many experts believe that number is approaching 95 percent. During the same period, text messaging also increased

dramatically. Between 2006 to 2008 alone, for example, the number of such messages sent in the United States went from 65 million to 357 million.

Safety and Secrecy

Accompanying the introduction of phones that appealed to teens were marketing strategies that encouraged parents to get their teens cell phones. (In the United States, no one under the age of eighteen can purchase a cell phone contract.) For example, service providers created "family plans" that made it easy for parents to add teens to their existing cell phone plans, and when parents expressed concern about the expense of text messaging, providers offered plans with unlimited text messaging for a flat monthly

Martin Cooper displays a prototype of the first handheld cellular telephone, a behemoth compared to today's small, sleek phones. Cooper used such a phone in April 1973 to make the world's first call from a mobile phone.

fee as well. (Today some plans also provide essentially unlimited Internet use.) Cell phone providers also produced advertisements showing the benefit of having a cell phone handy during an emergency or roadside breakdown in places where there are no landline telephones. The idea that cell phones increase personal safety convinced many parents to provide their teens with such phones.

These parents soon found that in addition to enabling calls for help, cell phones also increased the level of communication between themselves and their children. Teens were able to call to tell their parents where they were and what time they would be home without searching for a pay phone or other landline. Some also began calling their parents for advice—and texting them as well, once this feature became widespread. As psychologist Sherry Turkle, who has studied cell phone use among teenagers, says, "Now you have adolescents who are texting their mothers 15 times a day, asking things like, 'Should I get the red shoes or the blue shoes?'"[11]

Many parents appreciate this level of contact, but some psychologists have become concerned that it interferes with teens' building relationships with others besides their parents. However, teens say that the introduction of text messaging has made it easier for them to talk to their friends, and such conversations have an added benefit: Whereas phone calls can be overheard, text messages are relatively easy to keep private. As Rob Callender of Teenage Research Unlimited says, "It's a form of silent communication; they [teens] can do it whenever, they can do it fairly secretively."[12] He believes this secrecy is what has made text messaging so popular among teens.

As of the end of 2010, over 40 percent of teenagers with cell phones were reporting that the reason they wanted a phone was so they could send text messages. By this time, texting, like calling, had become associated with safety. In her book *The Parent's Guide to Texting, Facebook, and Social Media* Shawn Marie Edgington advises parents: "If your child is ever caught in an emergency situation, text messaging is the technology you want them to have immediate access to. The technology associated with mobile mes-

"Now you have adolescents who are texting their mothers 15 times a day, asking things like, 'Should I get the red shoes or the blue shoes?'"[11]

— Psychologist Sherry Turkle.

saging offers benefits that phone calls can't."[13] Edgington explains that it takes less battery power and signal strength to send a text message than a phone call and points out that because a text message is silent, it is safer to use in any situation in which a call for help might be dangerous if overheard by the wrong person.

Poor Grades

The ability to text silently anywhere, however, even when batteries and signal are low, also makes it possible for students to send messages during class, and this can lead to poor grades. For example, Christoffersen says of his daughter, who for a time sent more than three hundred texts a day while at school, "She went from A's and B's one semester to F's in two months."[14] Grades can also suffer when cell phone use takes the place of doing homework. This can occur because a student finds it hard to leave the phone off during study time, or it can occur because texting makes it easier for students to plan to socialize after school instead of studying. Antidrug experts say that texting has also become a common way for teens to arrange drug deals. All of these activities are reasons for adults to become concerned about teen texting.

Some educators argue that texting hurts language skills as well. The Education.com website reports, "Although controversial, yet another possible risk of text messaging is how it may contribute to increasingly poor spelling and writing skills in youth. Because texting uses intentionally misspelled words, nonstandard abbreviations, letter substitutions, and little or no punctuation, some educators believe it encourages poor literacy and a blunt, choppy style at odds with academic rigor."[15] On the other hand, some cell phones provide Internet access, which can offer educational benefits to students.

> "[Texting] is a form of silent communication; they [teens] can do it whenever, they can do it fairly secretively."[12]
>
> — Journalist Rob Callender, Director of Insights for Teenage Research Unlimited.

Internet Dangers

Although surveys indicate that less than one-fourth of teens have a phone that can access the Internet, this number is sure to grow. In 2011 alone, approximately 462 million new smartphones were shipped worldwide. Perhaps the most popular among teens is

Apple Inc.'s iPhone, introduced in January 2007. Cyber-crime expert Frederick S. Lane calls this device both "re-markable" and "troublesome for parents" because it has a "seductive combination of well-designed and powerful hardware, flexible software, and wireless connectivity."[16]

Lane notes that this phone and Apple's development of the iTunes Store in 2008, which sells phone applications (apps), can expose kids to inappropriate content and present them with opportunities to get into trouble online. He says,

> Although Apple has aggressively policed the iTunes Store to prevent the sale of obscene, inde-cent, and even politically provocative apps, there are still hundreds, even thousands, of iPhone (or Android or Blackberry) applications that can land kids in trouble. For instance, every major social network site—Facebook, MySpace, Twit-ter, etc.—has its own app for posting photos or comments, and dozens of third-party apps offer additional tools for interacting with those sites.[17]

Lane and others worry that kids accessing such sites and per-haps also posting photos there will encounter sexual predators. They point out that given the private nature of cell phones, it is harder to monitor teens' Internet use on a cell phone than it is on a computer. "Kids have this easy access to the internet so it makes it a lot harder for parents to supervise their internet use,"[18] says Internet safety expert Donna Rice Hughes. Cell phones also make it easy for online bullies, or cyberbullies, to harass people without being caught.

Harassment

Cyberbullies use cell phones to threaten or harass others via text messages, a behavior that communications expert Edgington calls textual harassment. She says that many teens are concerned about this problem, while many parents are not taking it seriously enough. She reports, "Today's headlines are full of children being virtually attacked by text message. They're being cyberbullied, threatened, and harassed on a daily basis, falling victim to the perils of the easy exchange of information that all mobile devices offer. Most parents are aware of the text harassment problem, but their first thought is to immediately dismiss the threat because it sounds impossible that their child could be involved."[19]

Other experts, however, counter that it is not the cell phone that is causing the problem, but the bully. This is also true of sexting, whereby a cell phone is used to share sexually suggestive or even pornographic pictures. The cell phone user is to blame for sending such images, not the phone itself, these experts contend. Nonetheless, the rapid communication that cell phones allow makes it easy to say or do something on impulse without considering the possible long-term consequences.

> "Today's headlines are full of children being virtually attacked by text message."[19]
>
> — Communications expert Shawn Marie Edgington.

Pocket Dialing

In some instances, however, the phone itself really is to blame for a miscommunication. This is true of pocket dialing, which became possible as cell phones evolved to include automatic dialing features. Pocket dialing occurs when, while a phone is tucked in its owner's pocket, an autodial key is accidentally pressed so that unbeknownst to the owner, the phone calls someone. These unintentional calls allow the receiver to hear conversations that the phone's owner might not want overheard, or it can have even more serious consequences. As digital expert Richard Guerry reports, "The recipient of the call usually receives a very annoying, long and potentially incriminating message. As smart phones evolve to become faster, and to more easily connect to the web, it becomes that much easier to pocket dial 'private' pictures, videos, files and texts to the Internet, other cell phones, email and more by accident!"[20]

Radiation Concerns

Pocket dialing is not the only way cell phones might be affecting users without their knowledge. Since the early days of cell phone technology, people have been worried that cell phones might cause cancer. This theory arises from the fact that wireless phones transmit via a low-frequency form of radiation of a type called nonionizing radiation. Also used for radar, AM/FM radios, and microwave ovens, nonionizing radiation has not been proved to cause cancer in humans. However, its cousin ionizing radiation—used for X-rays and radiation therapy—has been shown to cause cancer in humans who have been exposed to high amounts. Therefore some experts worry that repeatedly putting a cell phone near a human brain could be dangerous.

Support for this theory has its origins in the 1960s, when sci-

Worries about cell phones and radiation have existed for years. One concern is that holding a cell phone to one's ear can expose the brain to potentially dangerous amounts of radiation.

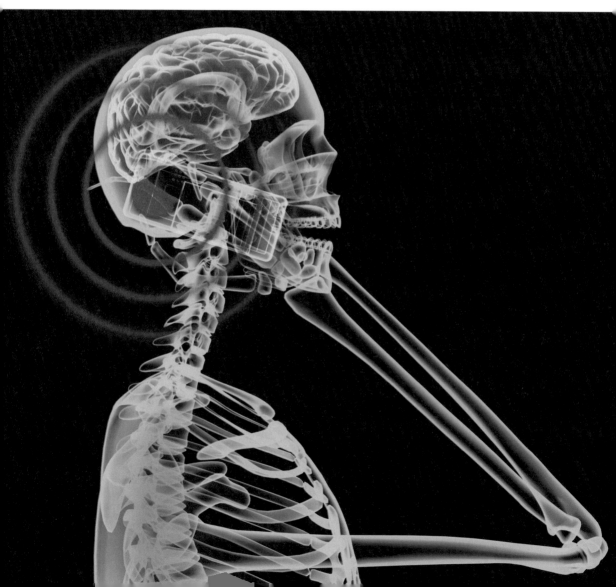

entists studying the radiation associated with radar began to believe it could be harmful to human brain cells. In 1967, when the first popular microwave oven hit the marketplace, scientists started worrying about microwave radiation, too. In the mid-1970s, studies into the effect of microwave radiation on brain cells showed that it is able to penetrate the barrier between the circulatory system and the brain in rats. This effect makes the environment of the brain unstable enough to harm nerve cells there.

The American public was largely unaware of this research until 1993, when David Reynard of Florida went on a popular talk show, *Larry King Live*, to argue that his wife's brain tumor had been caused by cell phone use. To draw attention to this issue, Reynard had recently filed a lawsuit against several companies that manufactured phones and provided cell phone service. The lawsuit was dismissed for lack of evidence in 1995, but by then the connection between cell phones and brain tumors was firmly fixed in the public mind.

Effect on Teens

Since Reynard's appearance, researchers have continued to study the effects of cell phone radiation, and many have concluded that long-term use can increase the risk of developing a tumor in the head, although the tumor might not be cancerous. Several studies have found no increased risk of brain tumors in people using a phone for three to five years, while studies released in 2010 have found that adults who use a cell phone for more than ten years are more likely than others to develop a brain tumor. However, no one has yet conducted a study on long-term use involving children and teens, despite the fact that some experts believe young people are at the most risk from cell phone radiation.

Keith Black, chairman of neurology at Cedars-Sinai Medical Center in Los Angeles, California, explains the reason for this belief: "Children's skulls and scalps are thinner. So the radiation can penetrate deeper into the brain of children and young adults." Black also suggests that cell phones could cause other types of damage besides tumors. He says, "What microwave radiation does in most simplistic terms is similar to what happens to food in mi-

Phone Plans

Cell phone plans typically require a cell phone user to sign a two-year contract agreeing to pay a certain amount per month in exchange for a certain number of user minutes for each category of use—talking, texting, and accessing data on the Internet. For example, in May 2012 a Sprint "Everything Data" family plan offered three thousand voice minutes, unlimited texting, and unlimited data at a cost of $169.99 for two cell phone lines. Using more than these three thousand minutes would cost the subscriber additional money; someone worried about this might choose a plan with unlimited voice minutes, but this is more expensive. Alternatively, users can buy a prepaid or pay-as-you-go phone for a flat fee. Such phones do not require a contract, but when the minutes run out, the phone will not work again unless more minutes are purchased. Many parents do not want their teens to have a prepaid phone because they fear the phone will run out of minutes right when it is needed most and because these phones do not allow parents to monitor their teens' cell phone use via a cell phone bill.

crowaves, essentially cooking the brain. So in addition to leading to a development of cancer and tumors, there could be a whole host of other effects like cognitive memory function, since the memory temporal lobes are where we hold our phones."[21]

Therefore, some experts say, young people should not use cell phones at all, or at least use them sparingly. Others say that young people should limit themselves to sending text messages rather than making calls, since texting keeps the phone much farther from the head. The cell phone industry—while continuing to insist that phones are safe—also advises users to keep the phone as far away from the head as possible. The most common recommendation is that phones be kept at least five-eighths of an inch away from the skull, but an even stronger recommendation is that a headset—a headphone combined with a microphone—be used instead. Some people think, however, that cell phones are simply too dangerous for young people to use even if they follow these precautions. For example, in May 2011 the World Health Organization (WHO) deemed cell phones to be as big a health risk for all ages as smoking cigarettes.

Nonetheless, lawsuits arguing that cell phone devices cause brain cancer or other illnesses continue to be unsuccessful, and in June 2011 the vice president of the Cellular Telecommunications Industry Association, John Walls, announced, "Based on previous assessments of the scientific evidence, the Federal Communications Commission has concluded that there's no scientific evidence that proves that wireless phone use can lead to cancer.'"[22] Consequently many people ignore warnings that cell phones might cause tumors.

In fact, teens typically ignore all concerns about their cell phone use. They even continue to use their phones under less than ideal circumstances, such as while suffering pain in their thumbs from too much texting. In addition, studies as recent as 2011 have found that despite media attention to the cost of using cell phones, only 66 percent of young people are concerned about keeping their phone bills down. This is because teens have other, more pressing concerns, including staying connected with one another and staving off boredom—both of which can be satisfied with cell phone use. Consequently the devices only grow more popular among teens each year.

Facts

- In a 2011 study by marketing expert Martin Lindstrom, when babies under the age of two were given a smartphone, they were immediately fascinated with it, and most touched the screen as though trying to turn it on.

- According to the Pew Research Center, in the United States 87 percent of African Americans and English-speaking Hispanics own a cell phone, compared to 80 percent of whites.

- According to the CTIA, the wireless industry trade association, the wireless industry made a total of $169.8 billion in 2011.

- CTIA reports that in 2011 cell phone users sent 2.30 trillion text messages.

- CTIA reports that in December 1996 there were 44 million wireless subscriber connections; in 2011 there were 331.6 million.

How Do Cell Phones Impact Personal Relationships?

Viewers of a 2010 episode of the MTV reality television show *16 and Pregnant* were stunned when teen mother Chelsea received a hostile text message from her infant daughter's father, Adam, calling her fat, worthless, and stupid. Many reacted by posting online comments criticizing Adam. Some added that they too had received hateful text messages from boyfriends or girlfriends. In fact, in a 2009 study conducted by MTV in partnership with the Associated Press, 12 percent of young people said that their boyfriend or girlfriend had said horrible things to them via texts or e-mails.

These people, however, undoubtedly did not have the benefit that Chelsea had of an audience reviewing their text messages. According to her father, these witnesses made a difference in how Chelsea reacted to the event. At a reunion episode of the TV show, he said that he believed Chelsea, who by then had broken up with Adam, would never again be in a relationship with Adam because, as blogger Cathy J. Wilson reports, "the world knew of the text message abuse and would be judging her if she went back with him."[23]

Deadly Consequences

Wilson applauds this response because she believes Chelsea's relationship with Adam could have become violent had it continued. But she also bemoans the fact that most other teens do not have an audience looking over their shoulders, pointing out that the private nature of texting often isolates people from friends who might prevent them from becoming victims. She explains, "The fact that text messages are nonverbal and therefore can be kept private and hidden is just one reason they are so dangerous when it comes to dating violence. At least if a friend is talking to a sig-

Phone Love

Martin Lindstrom, an expert on marketing psychology and the author of *Brandwashed: Tricks Companies Use to Manipulate Our Minds and Persuade Us to Buy*, believes that people who are compelled to use their cell phones are not addicted to them but actually in love with them. He came to this conclusion after conducting several experiments in which he studied how people reacted when exposed to cell phones, by observing them and scanning their brains. In one study, brain activity showed that people had a similar response when they were looking at pictures of Apple phones as when looking at pictures of religious images like rosary beads. In another, he discovered that in a test to determine which sounds most affected people, the top three sounds were the Intel chime (a popular ringtone), a giggling baby, and a vibrating cell phone. In a third study, when he exposed people between the ages of eighteen and twenty-five to the sound of a ringing or vibrating cell phone, he discovered via imaging scans that the part of the brain associated with feelings of love and compassion became extremely active. In fact, the test subjects reacted as though they were near a loved one.

nificant other on the phone, you can listen and gauge whether the conversation is escalating into dangerous territory. It's a lot more difficult to do that when your friend is silently texting."[24]

Gary Cuccia of Pennsylvania agrees. He blames texting for the reason no one realized that his sixteen-year-old daughter, Demi Brae, was in danger after breaking up with her boyfriend in 2007. "When I was growing up," he says, "we had one phone in the whole house, and if you were fighting with your girlfriend, everybody knew about it."[25] After the breakup, Brae's boyfriend texted her repeatedly in an attempt to get her back. "You know you can't live without me,"[26] he told her. After dozens of messages, Brae agreed to meet with him alone at her house, and when he got there he stabbed her sixteen times. He was later convicted of her murder and sentenced to life without parole.

Lynne Russell also blames texting for contributing to the death of her nineteen-year-old daughter Siobhan at the hands of her boyfriend, then-seventeen-year-old Lee Wiggins, in 2009. Wiggins stabbed the girl in the heart while they were in his bedroom, and after he was arrested her parents discovered that he had sent her dozens of disturbing text messages. Had these messages not been so private, Russell says, someone could have helped Siobhan realize that the relationship was dangerous. Indeed, many studies have shown that young people either have trouble recognizing that a relationship is risky or are too embarrassed to ask for help escaping such a relationship.

Constant Messaging

Sometimes it is not the private nature of text messages at issue but the fact that text messages can easily be sent over and over again, twenty-four hours a day. This constant messaging can be used as a form of control or abuse within a relationship. For example, in 2010 a sixteen-year-old girl in California received text messages around the clock, encouraging her to get back with her ex-boyfriend. Some of these texts came from the ex-boyfriend himself, but others came from four friends he had paid to take over the texting whenever he could not do it himself. In another 2010 case, the boyfriend of a young woman in Rockville, Virginia, demanded that she text him photos at specific times of the day, showing her exact location near a clock that displayed the time so that he would know the photo had just been taken.

According to the 2009 AP-MTV study, nearly one-fourth of young people in a romantic relationship report that their partner checks up on them several times a day, whether by phone calls, texts, or online messages, to find out what they are doing and who they are doing it with. More than 20 percent feel this activity is excessive. Some experts believe that this number would be much higher if not for the fact that many teens do not have a clear concept of what "excessive" might mean. As Amar Toor reports in an article on dating violence, because frequent texting is so common among teens, many "don't see a problem with receiving hundreds of texts a day," and this makes it "difficult for young targets to differentiate between normalcy and outright harassment."[27]

Nonetheless, experts who help teens deal with abusive relationships say they have to take their cues from the person receiving

Text messaging offers a quick and easy means of checking in with friends and family but it can also be overused or abused. Romantic relationships can be strained by texting excessively every day.

the texts as to whether a particular situation is abusive. Marjorie Gilberg, executive director of a group called Break the Cycle that combats dating violence, explains, "If you're getting 50 messages an hour and you want 50 messages an hour, that's not a problem. But if you're getting 50 messages an hour and you don't even want one, that's very different."[28]

Even so, according to Elizabeth Miller, an expert on teenage dating issues and also an assistant professor of pediatrics at the University of California at Davis School of Medicine, "We are identifying teen dating abuse and violence more than ever."[29] She also reports that in a recent study many eleven- to fourteen-year-olds whose boyfriends or girlfriends were harassing them by text stated that the texts often came between midnight and 5 a.m. when their parents were asleep.

Lack of Cues

Teens who insist on having their girlfriend or boyfriend answer the phone or respond to text messages no matter what time it is do so to exert control over their partner. Psychologist William S. Pollack of Harvard University says that his own research has shown that this behavior is more typical of boys. He says that "usually when adolescent boys get involved with girls, they fall into the societal model which we call 'macho,' where they need to show they are the ones in control" and that constantly texting and phoning a girl is often part of an effort "to gain control back."[30] Indeed, the National Teen Dating Abuse Helpline reports that many of its calls come from girls complaining about boys telling them what to do and what clothes to wear, and this has been true since the helpline was established in 2007.

But even when a relationship has no control issues, it can be damaged by text messaging. One reason this happens is that text messages are brief and lack the nonverbal cues that can indicate when the sender is using humor or sarcasm. This can cause misunderstandings and hurt feelings. On the subject of teen texting, the Pew Research Center found that many kids had trouble determining the emotions associated with the message, and that this difficulty often led them to call rather than text.

For example, in a 2010 study, one middle school girl told the

Teachers Connect

Cell phones can greatly improve the relationship between students and teachers not only by improving communication between the two but by giving students an easier way to complete assignments. One tool for doing both is a telecommunications service called Google Voice. Since 2009 this service provides users with a unique phone number that people can call to record messages for that person. Consequently an English teacher can tell students to call the number and recite poetry on the recording, for example, or a French teacher can ask students to repeat a list of vocabulary words that the teacher can subsequently listen to in order to be sure that students are learning what they need to learn. These voice recordings can also be downloaded and posted online, so that teachers can share particularly good work with other students. In addition, Google Voice can be used for conference calling, which means that groups of students can discuss classroom topics and record these discussions.

Pew researchers, "I like to talk [on the phone] because I like to hear, because sometimes on AIM [instant messaging] or texting I get mixed up from people's emotions. They'll be like, 'Oh stop talking to me,' and you don't know if they're joking or not joking. It's kind of annoying."[31] Similarly, high school student Jenna Welsh, in a column for the *Gettysburg Times* of Gettysburg, Pennsylvania, says, "A simple joke in a text could be misconstrued as an insult because the nonverbal communication just isn't there."[32] In addition, some teens are hurt when friends tell them personal information via text rather than in person, or at least in a phone call.

Response Time

Another reason that texts can unintentionally cause hurt feelings is related to the fact that even casual friends and acquaintances, not just boyfriends or girlfriends, expect texts to be answered right away. Mizuko Ito and Daisuke Okabe, who have researched text messaging patterns in Japan, explain that cell phones have created "the need to be continuously available to friends and lovers, and the need to always carry a functioning mobile device. These disciplines are accompanied by new sets of social expectations and manners. When unable to return a message right away, young people feel that a social expectation has been violated."[33] In other words, boyfriends can become angry with girlfriends, or vice versa, for not answering their text messages immediately, no matter where they are or what time it is.

The speed with which a text message is typically typed and sent can also cause problems in relationships, not just between boyfriends and girlfriends but among friends, classmates, and family members. The same is true of the ease with which people are generally able to reach others via a cell phone call. In either case, faster communication can lead to speaking without thinking. As Richard Guerry explains:

> Digital technology offers the ability for instant gratification and physical separation where digital citizens no longer have to "tell someone off" in their minds or wait to tell them to their face. With digital technology, citizens can tell someone off immediately from their desk, car, bed, wherever they are; whether the person they are upset with is around or not. People can lash out at whomever has upset them, just when they are at their angriest and have the most hurtful and malicious things to say. However, as is the case in any life situation, just because citizens *can* does not always mean that they *should*![34]

Bullying

Cell phones can also make bullying easier. Frederick S. Lane explains, "It takes mere seconds . . . for a kid to type out and send a three-word text message that can ruin a classmate's day. *You're so fat! Nobody likes you! Who dresses you? I hate you!* If those seem cruel or hurtful, rest assured that kids are capable of coming up with far worse."[35]

Lane acknowledges that such comments have always been made by one kid to another. But he argues that "our modern-day onslaught of electronic gadgetry" has made it more likely that such incidents will occur, and with greater impact. He says, "The new technology is fast, and it's effective at reaching a broad audience quickly," adding that "people are more apt to say mean things about someone when they don't have to face the victim of their taunts."[36]

Gossip

But texting can also bring people together. One of the ways it does this is by making it easier to gossip—and although gossiping can be destructive to the subject of the gossip, it also serves to bind the gossipers together. In his book *Txtng: The Gr8 Db8* David Crystal stresses "the important role of gossip in maintaining social networks."[37] In addition, he quotes Kate Fox as saying that her research subjects "found texting an ideal way to keep in touch with friends and family when they did not have the time, energy, inclination or budget for a 'proper' phone conversation or visit."[38]

Expert in child development and behavior Christopher McCarthy says that texting not only can help the average teen maintain social ties but also can help severely anxious teens in this area. As someone who deals with such teens in his therapy practice, he has found that forms of social networking like texting "can help them by providing some space and protection from potential, immediate negative feedback which would cause the teen to shutdown and withdraw." McCarthy adds that texting and social networking also allows anxious teens to feel free to disclose things about themselves that, in the long run, will improve their friendships and bring them more self-confidence and mental well-being. In addition, he says, texting can "break down barriers to communication, such as cliques, popularity, socio-economics, and physical separation. Kids who normally wouldn't speak to each other at school are now able to connect and build friendships."[39]

"It takes mere seconds . . . for a kid to type out and send a three-word text message that can ruin a classmate's day."[35]

— Cyberbullying expert Frederick S. Lane.

Parents' Role

McCarthy also suggests that if a teen does not have access to texting, he or she will have trouble fitting in with other teens. Consequently he encourages parents to provide their teens with cell phones, saying,

> In today's culture, if your teen does not have access to texting or Facebook, they could be completely left out of their community network. In my practice, I have seen teen's mental health improve by utilizing these means of communication. They have more friends, closer friends, and feel better about themselves. It contradicts what we first thought would happen years ago, that kids would become even more socially isolated, but it's true. They still need face-to-face interaction, but the use of these technologies can make that connection less difficult to initiate and maintain.[40]

Cell phones can enhance the parent-child relationship by giving parents a non-confrontational way to monitor the activities of their kids, although this can backfire if parents only use the phone to check up on whether homework or chores have been done.

Parents, too, can benefit emotionally from their teens' cell phone use. In a July 2011 article in the journal *Cyberpsychology, Behavior, and Social Networking*, researcher Robert S. Weisskirch reported on his study into how cell phone communication affected teens' relationships with their parents. The study focused on families that included at least one teenager age thirteen to nineteen who had owned and used a cell phone for at least six months. Weisskirch wanted to learn, among other things, whether too much calling between parents and teens could damage relationships. He discovered that on the contrary, when these calls were meant as a way to keep in touch, they actually improved the parent-child relationship regardless of frequency. Parents reported having a closer relationship with teens who checked in often to report their whereabouts or ask permission to do things. In addition, both parents and teens reported having an especially good relationship in cases of the teen who often called the parent to ask for advice and other kinds of support. Overall, communication improved when cell phones were used in this way.

> "When used appropriately, [cell phones] can be a great tool for connecting and staying in touch."[41]
>
> — Martha Filipic, an editor with Ohio State University Extension.

Conversely, according to both parents and teens, the parent-child relationship suffered in cases of a parent who tended to call a teen while upset or angry and/or to monitor how the teen was doing in regard to academic activities like homework. Both parents and teens reported having lower self-esteem after such calls. In cases of a teen who used the phone often to ask for his or her parents' guidance, however, whether on academic or nonacademic activities, both parents and teens had high self-esteem.

Weisskirch concluded that cell phones can enhance the parent-child bond while also providing parents with less confrontational ways to monitor teens' activities—as long as this monitoring is not done while the parent is angry or upset and as long as the focus is not solely on schoolwork. In fact, calls and texts between parents and teens need to be about advice, guidance, and positive communication far more than about whether the teen has done his or her homework. As Martha Filipic, an editor for Ohio State University Extension, says in summarizing the main points of Weisskirch's research:

"If you get your daughter a cell phone, make sure you don't use it solely to try to monitor her whereabouts and activities. That could backfire and damage your relationship. But when used appropriately, they can be a great tool for connecting and staying in touch."[41]

Shutting People Out

Paradoxically, cell phones can also enable users to shut others out. Naomi Baron, professor of linguistics at American University and the author of *Always On: Language in an Online and Mobile World*, explains:

> People have always found ways to avoid unwanted conversation: crossing the street when a person you don't want to talk with is approaching or hanging up the phone if your boyfriend's mother—rather than your boyfriend—answers. However, new online and mobile technologies increase the range of options at our disposal for choosing when we want to interact with whom. We check caller ID on our cell phones before taking the call. We block people on IM or Facebook. And we forward email or text messages to people for whom they were never intended.[42]

In studying the ways in which technology has influenced behaviors, Baron has found that rather than feeling guilty for ignoring calls or text messages from family or friends, young people feel empowered by their ability to shut people out whenever they want. She says, "Not one of them expressed any regrets or suspicion that such manipulation might be just plain rude. [They] rationalized that the individuals trying to contact them were not aware that their calls or messages were being ignored—so no harm was done. . . . [But] I suspect that if you ask the parents or friends whose attempts at communication were blocked, you would hear a different story."[43]

Similarly, relationship expert Karen Gail Lewis complains about cell phones being used to shut people out in person. She says,

"We check caller ID on our cell phones before taking the call. We block people on IM or Facebook. And we forward email or text messages to people for whom they were never intended."[42]

— Naomi Baron, professor of linguistics at American University.

<blockquote>
"This technology is now used to undermine relationships."[44]

—Relationship expert Karen Gail Lewis.
</blockquote>

In addition to helping people keep in touch, cell phones interfere with personal relationships, pushing people away. It's wonderful to be able to call your honey from wherever you are (although lovers certainly have found ways to do that long before cell phones). But how often have you seen friends walking down the street—with one talking on the phone? Or, families at a restaurant or social event, with everyone chatting but the father (or mother) separated by the cell? What is intended as a together activity gets interrupted when one of the people "goes away" via the cell phone. This technology is now used to undermine relationships.[44]

For cell phone users, though, this behavior is part of a no-win situation: Accept the call while out with others and risk upsetting one's companions, or ignore the call and risk upsetting the caller. Cell phones often present this sort of dilemma. The challenge for users is to establish boundaries with friends and family so that calls and texts do not come at inappropriate times, and to communicate well enough with others to avoid phone-caused misunderstandings that might damage relationships. Users also need to recognize that phones can be a tool of abuse, and here too they need to set boundaries or reach out to others for help. In this way, phone users can limit the degree of potential harm, while still enjoying the social benefits that cell phones provide.

Facts

- Females ages sixteen to twenty-four are more likely to be a victim of violence at the hands of a romantic partner than any other age group.

- According to an MTV survey, 22 percent of teens say that someone has told a lie about them either online or in a text message.

- Studies indicate that 63 percent of teens living in single-parent households and 45 percent of teens living with two or more adults have been bullied via text message or while online.

- The Pew Research Center reports that 48 percent of teens use their phones to discuss personal matters with all of their close friends, with half of all teens saying they have more than five close friends.

- The Teenage Research Institute reports that more than one in four teenage girls in a relationship have experienced repeated verbal abuse, and 71 percent of all teens say that boyfriends or girlfriends spreading rumors about them via cell phones or the Internet has been a serious problem.

CHAPTER THREE

Is Cell Phone Addiction a Problem?

A teacher in Vermont, Jerry Tillotson was discussing job interviews with eighth graders as part of a class on careers when he asked them whether they would answer their cell phone during an interview. "What I wanted to hear my students say," he later reported, "was 'I would turn my cell phone off before I went into the interview.'"[45] Instead, roughly 95 percent of the class said they would answer the phone.

"When I expressed my surprise with their response," Tillotson says, "they looked around at each other, squinting and puzzled, failing to understand why someone with the power to give you a job might be put off by the interview being interrupted by the phone call."[46] The students justified their response by saying the call might be an emergency. But Tillotson thinks they were simply too addicted to their phones to even think of leaving them off. He notes that students sometimes forget their homework, but they never forget their cell phones.

Panic Attacks

Most people know someone who is never without a cell phone. Most people also know someone who has carried on a cell phone conversation in public, perhaps even during a theater performance, or who has refused to stop texting in a place where cell phones are banned. Some experts believe that such behavior is no more than a matter of the user being too self-centered to care about bothering or harming others. Under this view, cell phone use is a choice. Others say cell phone use is a compulsion, encouraged by a society that expects people to be reachable by phone at any time. Because of this expectation, Karen Gail Lewis says, "Rather than turn off the phones when occupied, people keep them on at all times. They are *never* free. In effect, cell phones now burden, not free people."[47]

But for some cell phone users, the loss of a cell phone produces great anxiety. In March 2012 SecurEnvoy, an Internet security firm, revealed that in their study on cell phone users, conducted in the United Kingdom, 77 percent of people ages eighteen to twenty-four reported suffering from panic attacks whenever they were without their cell phones. The study also found that overall, 66 percent of people experience such attacks—an 11 percent rise from a similar study four years earlier.

These attacks can result in desperation to find the missing phone. Sometimes sufferers become so frantic for their phones that they fail to go to work, class, or other important events so that they can continue their search. Others worry so much about not being able to use a cell phone that they always carry more than one phone and an extra battery or their battery charger to ensure their phone will continue to function.

> *"Rather than turn off the phones when occupied, people keep them on at all times. They are never free."[47]*
>
> — Therapist Karen Gail Lewis.

Some users become anxious even when they have a working phone in their possession, fearing that they might miss a call by not responding quickly enough. Psychologist Michael Carr-Gregg of Melbourne, Australia, an expert in this behavior among teens, says that sufferers typically cannot even go to sleep without a working phone right beside them. He reports, "Many of my clients go to bed with their mobile phones while sleeping just like how one will have the teddy bear in the old days."[48]

Nomophobia

This type of anxiety is called nomophobia, or "no mobile-phone phobia," and psychologists say it is a growing problem not only in the United States but internationally. In addition, this growth is more rapid among young people than older ones, largely because in many countries, young people's reliance on cell phones is far greater than that of adults. For example, studies have shown that in Italy one-fourth of teens have more than one cell phone, in Hungary more than three-fourths of teens and children own cell phones, and in Great Britain 36 percent of college students say they could not live without their cell phones. Also in Great Britain, 7 percent of college students admit to having lost a job or relationship because of their cell phone use. In India, one in five college students suffer from cell phone–related anxiety.

Another reason that nomophobia is growing more rapidly among young people, experts say, is that today's young people are more at risk for developing it than members of previous generations. Carr-Gregg explains why: "This is the most tribal generation of young people. Adolescents want to be with their friends on a 24-hour basis."[49] In other words, today's young people have a greater need to be connected with their peers than did teens years ago.

Another expert, Sanjay Dixit, blames young people's increased adoption of smartphones for their being at greater risk of developing nomophobia. Professor and head of the Community Medicine Department at the Mahatma Gandhi Medical College in Indore, India, Dixit has studied cell phone use among Indian medical students. In his studies he found that the more time they spend on a phone, the more likely they are to suffer from cell phone–related anxiety. Smartphones, Dixit notes, encourage people to rely on their phones more heavily, because such devices can be used instead of a computer to go online. Other research has shown that women are more likely to develop nomophobia and that women text more than men do, also suggesting that the affliction is tied to amount of cell phone use. Similarly, people who report being lonely, bored, or anxious when they are alone—and therefore are more prone to call or text someone for companionship—are also more likely to develop nomophobia.

> "Many of my clients go to bed with their mobile phones while sleeping just like how one will have the teddy bear in the old days."[48]
>
> — Adolescent psychologist Michael Carr-Gregg.

Like Drugs or Alcohol?

Some experts believe that the severe anxiety associated with nomophobia indicates that cell phones can be an addiction just like

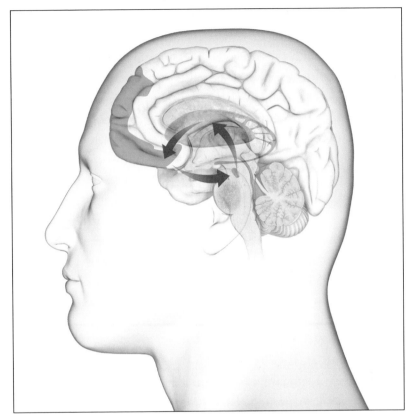

Some researchers believe that the ping or tone that signals the arrival of a text message prompts a chemical response in the pleasure center of the brain much like the effect of drugs in an addict. The chemical involved in this response is dopamine, which flows in the brain as indicated by the arrows.

drugs or alcohol. People addicted to these substances need to keep using the substances over and over again to feel good, typically increase their usage over time, and crave the item so much that they get upset when they cannot get their hands on it. All of these symptoms are associated with nomophobia as well. Consequently some clinics that specialize in the treatment of alcoholics or drug addicts have started treating cell phone "addicts" as well.

Nonetheless, experts disagree on whether people can have an actual addiction to cell phones. This disagreement stems from the fact that an addiction to drugs or alcohol, or certain foods with similar properties, can physically affect the brain. In cases of drug addiction, for example, the use of certain drugs can increase the amount of a chemical called dopamine in the brain, and the brain responds to this artificially induced increase by reducing the amount of dopamine it produces naturally. This means that the brain is now dependent on drugs for its normal level of dopamine—a chemical involved in such things as motivation, mood, memory, attention, and voluntary movement. As a result, without the drugs the person feels bad, and with the drugs the person feels good.

Some people believe cell phone use creates the same kind of pleasure. For example, Chris Cochran, a spokesperson for California's traffic safety office, says, "When there's a ping or tone [announcing a text message], it actually sets off a chemical response that mimics that of an addiction in the pleasure center of our brain. The brain says there's something good there and you have to see it."[50]

However, scientists have yet to determine conclusively whether the brains of people suffering from cell phone "addiction" really do show the same physical effects as someone addicted to drugs or alcohol. Consequently nomophobia is not currently included in the official guide to mental disorders, the *Diagnostic and Statistical Manual of Mental Disorders* (DSM), which includes addictions.

Dixit and other researchers believe that further studies into nomophobia, especially ongoing research into its possible physical effects, will eventually lead to its inclusion in the DSM. Proponents of DSM inclusion also point out that the psychological aspects of excessive cell phone use support the idea that nomophobia is a real addiction. As the Cellphone Addiction website notes, "If you continue a behavior despite mounting negative consequences, the behavior is likely addictive."[51] In the case of excessive cell phone use, these negative consequences can include financial hardship, relationship problems, and even physical injury.

"When there's a ping or tone [announcing a text message], it actually sets off a chemical response that mimics that of an addiction in the pleasure center of our brain. The brain says there's something good there and you have to see it."[50]

— Chris Cochran, a spokesperson for California's traffic safety office.

Distracted Walking

Studies indicate that as many as one-fourth of nomophobics are accident-prone. This is unsurprising given that such people have difficulty paying attention to anything but their phones. As a result, they often stumble, trip, fall, walk into things, or otherwise injure themselves while making calls or sending text messages. As examples, cases from the files of the Consumer Product Safety Com-

Institutionalized Addicts

One of the most internationally publicized cases of cell phone addiction involving young people occurred in 2009, when two children in Spain were confined in a mental institution because of their cell phone addiction. These children, ages twelve and thirteen, were sent there by their parents, who said the addiction had become so severe that the children could not function in school. They had also convinced relatives, without their parents' permission, to give them money to pay for their phone use. The children had had the phone for only eighteen months when they were institutionalized; for much of this time, their parents did not restrict their phone use at all. The children therefore typically spent six hours a day on their phones—talking, texting, or playing video-games. Maite Utges, director of the mental institution, said that the children's treatment would mark the first time his doctors had dealt with cell phone addiction. In interviews about the case, he warned parents not to let any child under the age of sixteen use a cell phone.

mission, a government agency charged with protecting the public from injuries related to product safety, include a twenty-one-year-old who crashed his bicycle while trying to text and a fifteen-year-old girl who suffered serious head and back injuries as a result of texting while riding a horse. In other cases, a thirteen-year-old girl suffered serious burns because she was trying to text while cooking, a man cut himself while simultaneously talking on the phone and carving a chicken, a teenager dropped a barbell on himself while trying to talk on the phone and lift weights at the same time, and a sixteen-year-old boy suffered a concussion because he walked into a telephone pole while texting. Other people have been hurt because they tried to text while in-line skating or operating machinery. Distracted walking has also caused the death of several people who accidentally stepped into traffic while texting.

Inattentional Blindness

Distracted walking has been the subject of several studies in recent years. One such study, conducted by psychology professor Ira Hyman of Western Washington University in Bellingham, Washington, sought to determine just how distracted a cell phone user can become. To evaluate this, Hyman asked one of his students to put on a clown costume and ride a unicycle on campus. He discovered that only 25 percent of people who walked past the clown while talking on a cell phone noticed him.

Hyman also discovered that more than double this number noticed the clown if they were having a conversation with a person walking beside them rather than with someone on a phone. He therefore concluded that the cell phone, not the conversation, was what caused them to fail to see something that should have been obvious—a phenomenon called inattentional blindness. Scientists have theorized that this "blindness" occurs because while talking on the phone, people create mental images of the person to whom they are speaking, and the brain has difficulty processing both imagined and real images at the same time.

In any case, inattentional blindness related to cell phone use is a growing problem. According to researchers at Ohio State University who studied the records of the Consumer Product Safety Commission, during the three-year period from 2006 to 2008, the number of emergency room visits related to distracted walking doubled each year. In 2008 this number was more than one thousand, roughly one-fourth of which involved people ages sixteen to twenty, and it is undoubtedly much higher today. In addition, countless cases involving bumps, bruises, or other minor injuries that do not warrant a trip to an emergency room go unreported.

Texting Tendonitis

Many cell phone "addicts" also suffer from repetitive stress injuries (RSIs), which are injuries resulting from repeated overuse of a particular body part. An RSI can cause tendonitis, the inflammation or irritation of a tendon, and this in turn can cause discomfort or pain as well as numbness. If left untreated, it also causes loss of muscle strength, because tendons attach muscles to bones.

The most common type of RSI associated with cell phone use is the result of excessive texting, due to the frequent, repetitive use of thumbs to press keys. But although the pain and inflammation typically start in the thumb and hand, they can spread to the fingers and the wrist. These body parts can cramp as well, and in severe cases the hands become disabled. Sufferers can also experience pain in the elbow and shoulder as the condition grows worse.

Roughly 20 percent of nomophobics suffer from RSI caused

Embarrassing Videos

Videos of people falling while texting sometimes make the evening news and often appear on YouTube and other online video-sharing sites. Many of these videos have been taken by friends or passersby, ironically, using cell phone cameras. Other videos are caught on security cameras or even by reporters broadcasting live on TV. In one incident from February 2012, for example, a woman falling on her face while texting appeared in the background of a live television news broadcast in Canada. In another incident in January 2011, a security camera caught a woman falling into a fountain while texting at the Berkshire Mall in Reading, Pennsylvania. After the mall's security guard posted this video on YouTube and it was picked up by the news media, the woman in the video, forty-nine-year-old mall employee Cathy Cruz Marrero, threatened to sue the mall for embarrassing her publicly, and the security guard was fired. However, no one knew the woman's identity until she went on a morning TV show on ABC, *Good Morning America*, to complain about being made a national laughingstock.

by texting. Doctors commonly refer to the condition as text message injury (TMI), BlackBerry thumb (named for the BlackBerry smartphone), or cell phone thumb. Recently the media has coined a new term for it: teen texting tendonitis, since far more teens than adults experience it.

Nerve Damage

Another type of phone-related RSI is cell phone elbow, caused not by texting but by talking on the phone. During phone conversations, people must keep their elbow bent at roughly 90 degrees to press the phone to the ear—unless they are using a hands-free device—and this position compresses a nerve in the elbow. If the pressure occurs repeatedly or over a long period of time, it can irritate the nerve to the point of causing elbow and shoulder pain, along with numbness or tingling in the ring finger and little finger of the afflicted arm. It can also cause muscle weakness and such a deterioration of coordination and mobility that sufferers cannot hold on to things without dropping them. At this point surgery is often necessary to repair the nerve—and if the nerve is left untreated, the ring and pinky fingers can become clawlike.

Painful Muscles and Joints

Talking or texting on a cell phone can also affect the way people stand, sit, and walk, and these changes in posture can cause aches and pains in the neck, back, and shoulders. Orthopedic surgeon Alton Barron of St. Luke's–Roosevelt Hospital in New York, who has seen patients with such problems, says that texting in particular can cause upper body pain because "we are straining our muscles both in our necks and our upper backs and our shoulders to accommodate for this position [required for texting]."[52]

In fact, researchers say that cell phones are responsible for the fact that neck and shoulder pain is becoming more common on college campuses. According to a study by Judith Gold, an assistant professor of epidemiology at Temple University's College of Health Professions and Social Work, males are more susceptible to this pain, although the reason is not yet clear. Gold also says that texting is causing the kind of physical damage in young people that used to be seen only in adults who have spent years hunched over office computers. This is not only because of the many hours that young people text but because "the way the body is positioned for texting—stationary shoulders and back with rapidly moving fingers—is similar to the position for typing on a computer."[53]

Excessive texting can also damage joints in young people in ways that might continue to cause pain years later. According to a 2011 study at the NYU Hospital for Joint Diseases in New York involving students aged nine to fifteen, just two hours a day of texting caused joint damage. Rheumatology professor Yusuf Yazici, who oversaw the research, says, "Our study has shown the negative impact that . . . using mobile phones can have on the joints of young children, raising concerns about the health impact of modern technology later in life."[54] Yazici further found that the younger the individual the more pain they experienced, and that girls experienced more pain than boys. In addition, among all groups, the chances of having pain doubled with every additional hour of texting.

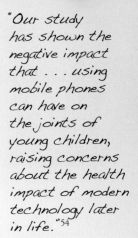

"Our study has shown the negative impact that . . . using mobile phones can have on the joints of young children, raising concerns about the health impact of modern technology later in life."[54]

— Rheumatology professor Yusuf Yazici.

Sleep Problems

Researchers also know that excessive cell phone use can cause sleep problems, especially when this use occurs within an hour before bedtime. Some experts blame such difficulties on the increase in brain activity caused by cell phones, saying it creates the same wide-awake state as drinking coffee before bed. Others say that the lighting is the problem, since exposure to artificial light—from a television screen, cell phone display, or computer monitor, for example—can make the body think it is daytime. Charles Czeisler, a professor at Harvard Medical School and chief of the Division of Sleep Medicine at Brigham and Women's Hospital, explains how this affects people: "Artificial light exposure between dusk and the time we go to bed at night suppresses release of the sleep-promoting hormone melatonin, enhances alertness and shifts circadian rhythms to a later hour—making it more difficult to fall asleep."[55]

Excessive cell phone use, especially around bedtime, can contribute to sleep problems. Surveys suggest that many teens use their phones to talk or text late into the night even on school nights.

A study released by the National Sleep Foundation in March 2011, which polled over fifteen hundred Americans between the ages of thirteen and sixty-four, found that 60 percent of those polled are dissatisfied with the amount and/or quality of their sleep nearly every night, and 95 percent are exposed to light-emitting screens in the hour before bed at least a few times a week. In addition, more than half of the young people polled report that they get or send text messages every night or nearly every night. Commenting on this study, Czeisler says, "Invasion of such alerting technologies into the bedroom may contribute to the high proportion of respondents who reported that they routinely get less sleep than they need."[56]

More Important than Sleep

For many people, however, using their cell phones is more important than sleep. In studying how cell phone use affects sleep in young people ages thirteen to fifteen, for example, scientists at

Katholieke University Leuven in Belgium found that the later past their bedtimes the teens used their cell phones, the more tired they were the next day. Nonetheless, 60 percent continued to use their cell phones, either to talk or to text, late into the night—some even past 3 a.m. on a school night. Other studies have produced similar findings. Consequently, Russell Rosenberg, vice chairman of the National Sleep Foundation, says, "Unfortunately cell phones and computers, which make our lives more productive and enjoyable, may also be abused to the point that they contribute to getting less sleep at night leaving millions of Americans functioning poorly the next day."[57]

Yet, as do other problems related to excessive cell phone use, sleep problems fail to convince cell phone "addicts" that it might be better to put the phone away. Moreover, people who rely heavily on their cell phones often insist that their use is not excessive, and that even if it is, there is no reason to cut it down. Many also say that they can do without their phones any time they want to but when dared to prove this, they cannot. However, experts continue to disagree about whether this behavior reflects a genuine addiction or simply a bad habit.

Facts

- The Pew Research Center reports that only one-third of people aged sixty-five and over keep a cell phone near their bed during the night.

- A recent survey by the Pew Internet and American Life Project found that 51 percent of cell phone users felt they would have a hard time giving up their cell phones.

- Because of the risk of cell phone addiction, experts advise parents to delay getting their children a phone for as long as possible.

- In August 2011 the results of a survey conducted by the communications company Ofcom in the United Kingdom revealed that among British smartphone users, 37 percent of adults and 60 percent of teen owners said they are extremely addicted to their phones; 22 percent of the adults and 47 percent of the teens admitted to talking on the phone while on the toilet.

- Addiction counselors routinely advise people troubled by excessive cell phone use to set aside one day per week as a "no texting" or "no calling" day.

CHAPTER FOUR

How Serious a Problem Is Cell Phone Use While Driving?

In December 2011 a jury in Florida's Miami-Dade County awarded more than $8.8 million to the family of Myriam del Socorro, a woman killed by a teenager texting while driving. Three years earlier, Del Socorro had been a passenger in a car driven by her husband when seventeen-year-old Luis Cruz-Govin rammed into it. Cruz-Govin had been driving over 60 miles per hour (mph) (96.5 kmh) in a 40 mph (64kmh) zone while texting his girlfriend.

Unfortunately, such situations are not rare. According to the National Safety Council, in 2011 at least 23 percent of all traffic crashes—or at least 1.3 million—involved cell phone use, and the National Highway Traffic Safety Administration has found that 25 percent of all police-reported traffic accidents are either directly or indirectly caused by driver inattention. Other studies have found that cell phone users between the ages of sixteen and nineteen are responsible for over 20 percent of fatal car crashes in the United States. However, even more fatalities might actually be related to cell phone use because, unlike situations in which a driver is drunk or on drugs, it is difficult for police to tell whether a driver was texting or talking on the phone at the time of the accident.

Distracted Driving

Phone records showed that Cruz-Govin sent one hundred twenty-seven texts on the day of the accident, one of them just two minutes before paramedics were called to the crash site. This evidence, along with testimony that Cruz-Govin was a habitual texter, helped lead to his guilty verdict. In addition, David L. Strayer, a professor of psychology at the University of Utah, testified that Cruz-Govin's was a classic case of distracted driving, caused by the same inattentional blindness that causes distracted walking. Strayer, one of the leading experts on inattentional blindness, reports: "Our studies have found that the odds of getting into an accident [for a distracted driver] are . . . about eight times greater than for a non-distracted driver."[58] Another study, by the National Transportation Safety Board in 2011, suggests that texting while driving increases the risk of an accident by 2,300 percent.

Strayer says that talking on the phone, even a hands-free one, can also cause problems because both texting and talking require a person to think of things to say—unlike listening to the radio, which Strayer says is far less dangerous because it is a passive activity. Strayer has found that "cell-phone conversations made drivers more likely to miss traffic signals and react more slowly to the signals that they did detect." Moreover, "when a driver becomes involved in a cell-phone conversation, attention is withdrawn from the driving environment necessary for the safe operation of the vehicle."[59]

Among most drivers, conversing with a passenger in a car does not present the same attention deficit, because this conversation takes place within the driving environment. That is, as the driver and passenger talk, the passenger is aware of the conditions inside and outside the car and will react to them, thereby encouraging the driver to react as well. However, a study released in May 2012 by the Automobile Association of America (AAA) found that a sixteen- or seventeen-year-old driver's risk of having a fatal car accident per mile driven, even when the driver is not using a cell

"Our studies have found that the odds of getting into an accident [for a distracted driver] are . . . about eight times greater than for a non-distracted driver."[58]

— David L. Strayer, professor of psychology at the University of Utah.

phone, increases 44 percent if the passenger is also a teenager; the risk doubles if two teen passengers are in the car and quadruples with three teen passengers. This is because a teen passenger can be just as distracting to a teen driver as a cell phone.

Multitasking

Strayer's research has shown that teens generally have far more trouble than adult drivers when trying to drive and do anything else at the same time. This is because, he says, "they're just learning how to drive, so some of the things that a more experienced driver might have automated or become habitual are still quite effortful for a teen driver . . . they're also probably the most likely to be multitasking, either using a cell phone, or an iPod, or text messaging."[60]

In a 2011 study involving college students, Strayer and other researchers at the University of Utah found that the driving performance of 97.5 percent of the students fell 20 to 30 percent

Teen cell phone users who text or talk while driving are responsible for more than 20 percent of fatal car accidents in the United States. Cell phones are a growing problem in the hands of distracted drivers of all ages.

when they tried to talk on a cell phone while operating a driving simulator. The remaining 2.5 percent saw no drop in ability. Strayer calls these people supertaskers and stresses that they are extremely rare.

Talking Versus Texting

Other research has focused on the issue of driving and texting, which statistics suggest is far less dangerous than talking on the phone. According to the National Safety Council in 2011, for example, out of over 1.3 million crashes, only about one hundred thousand can be directly connected to texting as opposed to other types of phone use. The group currently estimates that cell phone conversations are involved in twelve times as many crashes as texting.

However, these statistics, like many others related to distracted driving, might not give a true picture of the problem. If the number of hours that people spend talking on the phone while driving is much higher than the number of hours spent texting, then this would account for the fact that when an accident happens, the driver is far more likely to be talking on the phone than texting. No surveys have yet provided reliable statistics on just how many people text versus talk on the phone while driving, but it is reasonable to assume that talking is far more common, given that the majority of people old enough to drive are in the age category more likely to talk than text.

Several studies have been conducted on how texting affects driving. For example, in October 2011 the Texas Transportation Institute of Texas A&M University released the results of a study that evaluated the reaction times of forty-two drivers, ages sixteen to fifty-four, who were navigating a vehicle on an 11-mile test track (17.7km). These drivers were tested under two conditions. They drove the track once without distractions and a second time while sending and receiving text messages.

Each time, they were told to stop whenever a yellow light flashed, and each time the researchers measured how quickly they responded. By the end of the test, researchers had discovered that texting added three to four seconds to the reaction time of driv-

Crash Violence

In 2009 filmmaker Peter Watkins-Hughes of the United Kingdom (UK) created a shockingly graphic video in an attempt to convince teens not to text while driving. In this video, starring teenage actors from Wales, a girl named Cassie takes her eyes off the road to look at her cell phone, and before she can look back up again she crashes into another car, killing four people. Shown in slow-motion with bloody details, the crash and its aftermath were simulated with the help of police officers, ambulance drivers, and firefighters, and afterward several school districts in Wales decided to show the film to high school students. But while people in the UK were supportive of this education effort, pundits in the United States complained the video was too graphic and gory to show to young people. The online video website YouTube, where a copy of the film was posted, restricted its viewing to people over the age of eighteen—thereby making it impossible for a large portion of its intended audience to view it.

ers—if they managed to stop at all. While either reading or sending a text, a driver was eleven times more likely to drive right past the light, often not even noticing it. The head of the study, Christine Yager, concludes, "Essentially texting while driving doubles a driver's reaction time. That makes a driver less able to respond to sudden roadway dangers."[61]

Texting Worse than Drunk Driving?

Another texting-while-driving test, conducted by *Car and Driver* magazine, gauged not only reaction time in response to a red light but how far the cars traveled before coming to a complete stop and whether the drivers stayed in their lanes during the test. It also tested each driver at two speeds, 35 mph (56kmh) and 70 mph (112kmh), and it compared the effects of driving while texting to the effects of driving while legally drunk but not using a cell phone.

There were only two test subjects, twenty-two-year-old Jordan Brown and thirty-seven-year-old Eddie Alterman, but the results are still enlightening. They showed that both men had as much or more trouble stopping within a safe distance while using a cell phone as they did while drunk. During one series of efforts, for example, at 35 mph (56kmh) Brown's car traveled an additional 21 feet (6.4m) past his normal stopping point while he was reading a message and an additional 16 feet (4.9m) while texting, but his reaction time was nearly the same while drunk but not texting. At 70 mph (112kmh), he went an additional 30 feet (9.1m) while reading a message, an additional 31 feet (9.5m) while texting, and an additional 15 feet (4.6m) when drunk.

At 35 mph (56kmh) Alterman went an additional 45 feet (13.7m) while reading a message, an additional 41 feet (12.5m) while texting, and an additional 7 feet (2.1m) while drunk. At 70 mph (112kmh), whether reading or sending a text, Alterman's best effort after several tries still resulted in his car going more than 90 feet (27.4m) farther than his normal stopping distance. In one of his tries, he traveled 319 feet (97.2m) past where he should have stopped. Moreover, according to Michael Austin, auto and airline industry reporter for *Car and Driver*, Alterman typically had his eyes off the road for an average of more than four seconds while texting, and he often drifted or veered out of his lane. Both men sometimes failed to notice the red light.

As a whole, the data suggest that a driver's reading a text or an e-mail on a phone adds roughly 36 feet (11m) to the car's stopping distance, and a driver's sending a text adds 70 feet (21.3m). In contrast, a legally drunk driver will take an average of just 4 feet (1.2m) longer than normal to come to a stop. Austin warns that although the study makes drunk driving look relatively safe, this is definitely not the case. He says, "Don't take the intoxicated results to be acceptable just because they're an improvement over

"Holding the phone up above the dashboard and typing with one hand would make it difficult to do anything except hit the brakes."[63]

— Michael Austin, technical editor for *Car and Driver* magazine.

the texting numbers. They only look better because the texting results are so horrendously bad. The [drunk] Jordan [Brown] had to be told *twice* which lane to drive in, and in the real world, that mistake could mean a head-on crash. And we . . . only measured response to a light—the reduction in motor skills and cognitive power associated with impaired [drunk] driving weren't really exposed here."[62]

Moreover, Austin believes that the drivers' results would likely have been much worse under real-world driving conditions. He explains, "We were using a straight road without any traffic, road signals, or pedestrians, and . . . Brown's method of holding the phone up above the dashboard and typing with one hand would make it difficult to do anything except hit the brakes. And if anything in the periphery required a response, well, both drivers would probably be [in serious trouble]."[63]

Phil LeBeau, auto and airline industry reporter for CNBC news, agrees that this test should not make people assume that

Studies suggest that texting and driving is at least as dangerous as drinking and driving—and maybe even more. When texting drivers take their eyes off the road, even a few seconds is long enough to veer into another car or miss a red light.

drunk driving is okay. But he also says that the results suggest texting and driving might be even more dangerous than drinking and driving. LeBeau decided to take the test himself but without the alcohol consumption, to see how he would do. He reports, "When I took the test for . . . texting, I was just as slow to react [as the *Car and Driver* test subjects]. On average, it took me four times longer to hit the brake. Mike Austin at *Car and Driver* told me in blunt terms that I was 'way worse' than the average driver."[64]

Memory Problems

Research shows that using a cell phone while driving can affect memory as well as reaction time. For example, Strayer has found that even when road signs are pointed out to a driver talking on a hands-free cell phone, the driver quickly forgets having seen the signs. Strayer reports that his test subjects "were more than twice as likely to recognize roadway signs" when they were driving without the distraction of a cell phone and were "less likely to remember them [the signs] if they were conversing on a cell phone."[65]

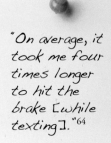

"On average, it took me four times longer to hit the brake [while texting]."[64]

— Phil LeBeau, auto and airline industry reporter at CNBC.

Other studies have shown that phone-related memory struggles can diminish performance. For example, one study showed that drivers trying to recall a phone number while driving had problems staying in their traffic lane. Another showed that trying to use a speech-based system to respond to an e-mail caused a 30 percent increase in the length of time it took to stop a car. Still another study found that memorizing and reciting a list—the way someone might do while trying to remember a grocery list dictated by a family member during a phone call—could diminish a driver's steering ability and braking time. The longer the list, the more trouble the driver had keeping the car in its lane.

Not Taken Seriously

Nonetheless, surveys show that the public does not take the issue of cell phone use behind the wheel seriously enough. As LeBeau says, "The American public correctly views drinking and driving as wrong. But when it comes to texting and driving, we are not as outraged. Probably because many of us have done it and still do it . . . [even where it's banned]. Sadly, it will likely take more accidents and more deaths to change that attitude. There are countless stories of teens dying in accidents because the driver was texting while driving."[66]

The Impossible Test

In May 2012 a video of an impossible driving test gained widespread attention in the media. Created and uploaded to YouTube by a Belgian group called Responsible Young Drivers (RYD) as part of a campaign to combat texting while driving, the video shows young drivers struggling to navigate a test track while texting. Participants were tricked into believing that a law had just been passed requiring them to prove that they were capable of driving well while texting. They were then told to type a message on a cell phone, as dictated by the tester sitting beside them in the passenger seat, while driving around the track and navigating through a series of cones. By all measures, the results were disastrous. Not one person "passed" the test; several gave up in despair without completing it; and one caused the instructor to hit his head on the dashboard after inexplicably slamming on the brakes while attempting to text.

Austin points out that part of the problem is that most people misjudge just how competent they are behind the wheel. He says, "In our test [for *Car and Driver* magazine], neither subject had any idea that using his phone would slow down his reaction time so much. Like most folks, they think they're pretty good drivers. Our results prove otherwise, at both city and highway speeds. The key element to driving safely is keeping your eyes and your mind on the road. Text messaging distracts any driver from that primary task."[67]

Laws Against Cell Phone Use While Driving

But while the general public is only just beginning to understand that texting while driving is a problem, lawmakers are increasingly addressing the issue. As of late 2012, ten states plus Washington, DC, Guam, and the Virgin Islands prohibit talking on a handheld phone while driving, and thirty-three states and Washington, DC, prohibit new drivers from talking on a hands-free phone while driving. (In defining a "new" driver, some cite the driver's age while others say it depends on the number of months the person has been driving and whether the person has a regular license or a learner's permit.) No state currently bans both handheld and hands-free phone use for all drivers, although in nineteen states and Washington, DC, it is illegal for a school bus driver to use a cell phone while passengers are on the bus.

Also as of late 2012, thirty-nine states, as well as Washington, DC, and Guam, have made it illegal for any driver, regardless of age or number of years behind the wheel, to send or receive text mes-

States have passed a variety of laws that restrict cell phone use while driving. In New York, Governor Andrew Cuomo (pictured) signs a Distracted Drivers bill in 2011. The bill allows police to stop motorists spotted texting while driving.

sages while driving. An additional six states prohibit new drivers from texting, and a few states fine drivers for texting if the texting leads the driver to commit some other traffic violation. In some states, authorities have passed local laws against various kinds of distracted driving, but in other states such laws are forbidden. In addition, Ohio is currently working to ban texting while driving for both adults and teens; however, although adults would still be allowed to use cell phones for purposes other than texting, teens under eighteen would be banned from using any electronic communications device while driving except in a verifiable emergency.

A Federal Ban

Because of the inconsistencies in laws from state to state, in April 2012 US transportation secretary Ray LaHood called for a federal law banning talking or texting on a cell phone while driving anywhere in the United States in any kind of vehicle. LaHood also warned car manufacturers that installing hands-free communication technology into new cars might not be a wise idea, since his department might eventually decide that these devices distract drivers enough to warrant being banned too. LaHood insists that the new law would reduce dangerous behavior much in the same way that drunk driving laws did once they began to be aggressively enforced, saying, "It used to be that if an officer pulled you over for drunk driving, he would pat you on the back, maybe call you a cab or take you home, but he wouldn't arrest you. Now that has changed, and the same enforcement can work for people who talk on cell phones while driving."[68]

The National Motorists Association, however, rejects the idea that such a law is needed. The association argues that public education efforts, particularly among young people, are the best way to reduce cell phone use while driving, just as such efforts have educated the public about the dangers of drunk driving and speeding. The association also argues that instead of banning only one form of driving distraction, efforts need to be made to educate the public about the many forms of distractions that exist today, so that they can learn to make wise choices about what they should and should not do while operating a motor vehicle.

Also opposing a federal ban on cell phones is Horace Cooper of the National Center for Public Policy Research. He argues that cell phone use should not be compared to alcohol use because, he believes, one is essential and the other is not, and therefore any law that equates the two is misguided. He says, "Treating cell phone use like drunk driving is particularly wrong-headed and assumes that cell-phone use and accessibility are casual novelties instead of the critical 21st century tool most Americans rely on. Unlike Washington, adults all across America understand the difference between responsible use of their cell phone and alcoholic misuse."[69]

Nonetheless, studies have shown that cell phone bans do reduce accidents. A March 2012 study by the University of California at Berkeley showed that four years after the state banned hand-held cell phone use while driving, the number of deaths caused by highway accidents had fallen by 22 percent, and highway fatalities directly connected to the use of a cell phone had fallen 47 percent. Commenting on California's success with its cell phone law, Jill Bentz of the West Virginia Insurance Federation says that such laws are similar to those enacted to combat speeding or to ensure that people riding in a car are protected by seat belts and car seats. She says, "These laws are a statement of our values and our reflection of a general consensus as to what [behaviors] we think are unacceptable."[70]

Awareness

Bentz supports the passage of a law like California's in her own state, saying it will not only save lives and reduce insurance claims but also help people understand how dangerous cell phones can be. She says, "Passing this law is going to heighten the awareness that people shouldn't be texting and people shouldn't be talking without hands-free equipment."[71] But some experts point out that a heightened awareness does not necessarily guarantee changes in behavior.

As evidence of this, in Nevada many drivers continue to use their cell phones while driving despite a well-publicized law enacted January 1, 2012, prohibiting this behavior. As of May 2012, according to the state's Office of Traffic Safety, nearly four thousand drivers have received tickets for breaking the law, and some were repeat offenders. One of the main reasons for this, according to authorities, is that when the phone rings, some drivers cannot seem to stop themselves from answering it. Consequently Erin Breen of Safe Nevada Partnership, which supports the new law, recommends: "If you can't drive without using your phone, lock it in your trunk when you get in the vehicle because no message or phone call is worth a life."[72]

But in the comments sections of articles about the new law, many Nevadans say they are going to continue to text and talk on the phone regardless of the risk of getting a ticket. For example, at a local Fox News website, a woman calling herself simply "Jane" writes, "This is a [stupid] law seriously! ima continue talking and textin while driving!! its called MULTITASKING!"[73] Law enforcement officials admit that catching scofflaws like "Jane" will be hard to do, especially since it is relatively easy to use a cell phone without anyone outside the car noticing.

Consequently many experts believe that the enactment of laws to combat using cell phones while driving should be accompanied by aggressive educational efforts. These efforts, researchers say, need to focus on getting people to understand just how rare it is for drivers to be able to multitask without putting themselves at great risk for a fatal accident. They also need to promote messages like that of California Highway Patrol officer Miguel Duarte of Moorpark, California. In talking to high school students about safe driving practices, he tells them to look at the last text message they received on their cell phone. After that, he reports: "Then I say, 'Is that text worth you dying?' because it only takes a split second."[74]

"If you can't drive without using your phone, lock it in your trunk when you get in the vehicle because no message or phone call is worth a life."[72]

— Erin Breen of Safe Nevada Partnership.

Facts

- In a 2011 poll, about 13 percent of adult drivers admitted to having surfed the Internet while driving.

- One-third of drivers admit to having sent or received text messages while driving; most say they do it only occasionally, but 18 percent do it regularly.

- According to researcher David L. Strayer, his studies suggest that 50 percent of teens text while driving.

- Studies conducted by the University of Utah suggest that 98 percent of Americans are significantly impaired when they try to multitask using a cell phone.

- According to the Virginia Tech Transportation Institute, immediately after reaching for a cell phone a truck driver is 5.9 times more likely to be involved in a crash, whereas other drivers are only 1.4 times more likely to crash.

- In a 2011 Harris Interactive poll, nine out of ten American adults said they support a ban on texting while driving.

CHAPTER FIVE

How Serious a Problem Is Sexting?

I n 2011 Charlie and Donna Witsell sued a Florida school district because school officials never warned them that their thirteen-year-old daughter, Hope, was suicidal. Just before the end of the school year in June 2009, having noticed that the girl was depressed and suspecting that she was cutting herself, school officials made Hope sign a "no harm" contract, vowing that she would tell an adult if she ever felt bad enough to kill herself. But they never told her parents about the contract.

The school also never told the Witsells that Hope was being tormented by classmates because of a photo she had texted to her boyfriend, Alex Eargood, showing her naked breasts—a photo that another girl, who had borrowed the boy's phone, then texted to students not only at her own school but six others nearby. Those students then texted it to friends and classmates, and eventually school officials found out about the photo. Hope was suspended for a week, with her parents' knowledge, but the bullies who called her names like "slut" and wrote hateful things about her on her MySpace page were never punished, and their brutal comments continued even after school started again in September 2009. Just days later, Hope hanged herself in her bedroom.

A Growing Problem?

This case illustrates the most serious consequence of using a cell phone to text a nude, partially nude, or otherwise sexually suggestive photo or video, a practice known as sexting. In a Harris online poll in 2009, the year that Hope committed suicide, one-fifth of the teens surveyed—including 9 percent of thirteen-year-olds—admitted to having sexted a naked picture of themselves or someone else. In surveys conducted the following year, that number had grown to roughly one-third.

Some experts believe that even more teens have probably sexted, since this activity is not something that teens are likely to admit to pollsters. But others argue that sexting might be far less prevalent than reported because of flaws in the way studies of teen sexting have been conducted. Specifically, what constitutes sexting can be poorly defined, and statistics can lump younger teens in with older ones more likely to be sexually active, making it seem as if fifteen-year-olds engage in the practice to the same degree as eighteen-year-olds.

In a 2010–2011 study, researchers at the University of New Hampshire attempted to get a more accurate view of the sexting problem by narrowing the definition of sexting to exclude cases of harmless sexual exploration and accidental sharing. For example, one case the researchers chose to exclude was that of a ten-year-old boy who sent a nude picture of himself to an eleven-year-old girl to upset her, and another involved a sixteen-year-old girl who sent a nude photo unintentionally to a boy who then passed it on. During telephone surveys of teens throughout the United States, malicious intent was key to determining which incidents were deemed sexting. In a separate but related study, the researchers used police records from 2008 and 2009 to determine the kind of sexting cases that law enforcement officials across the United States considered serious enough to warrant arrest and prosecution.

Ultimately, this study—which considered photos shared online via computer as a type of "sexting"—concluded that only 1 percent of young people ages ten to seventeen have intentionally shared, via computer or cell phone, nude pictures that would be considered graphic. The same percentage have shared pictures that would be considered suggestive but not necessarily graphic. The study also found that 7 percent of young people ages ten to seventeen have received a graphic or suggestive picture via some form of sexting.

Researchers also learned that in 2008 and 2009 fewer than four thousand incidents of sexting were reported to police nationwide.

Harmless or Harmful?

When the study was released in 2011, some people lauded it for providing a more realistic picture of the sexting phenomenon. For example, Michael Rich, director of the Center on Media and Child Health at Children's Hospital Boston, says that the study sheds light on an issue "about which we as a society have gotten pretty hysterical about and probably blew out of proportion." Rich adds that what adults call sexting is typically, among kids, a harmless sort of sharing. "We've been doing that since somebody scribbled a picture of a nude woman on the side of a cave and the guys gathered around to check it out."[75]

Others, however, say that what an adult perceives as harmless might not be perceived that way by a young person. In the University of New Hampshire study, for example, the researchers who excluded the incident of the ten-year-old boy who admitted to sexting an eleven-year-old girl saw it as just sexual play. But critics point out

Experts differ on how widespread the practice of sexting is among teens. While many teens would never consider sending nude photos of themselves to friends, others have experimented with sexting—sometimes with disastrous results.

Wrongful Prosecution

In a major case of wrongful prosecution connected to sexting, sixty-year-old high school assistant principal Ting-Yi Oei of South Riding, Virginia, was arrested in 2008 as a direct result of confiscating a sixteen-year-old student's phone because it contained a sexted image of a girl covering her bare breasts with her hands. A few weeks earlier, a co-worker suggested he save the evidence by transferring it to his computer, but being ignorant about technology, he had someone help him transfer it to his phone instead. When the student later got in trouble again, Oei brought up the previous incident in a conference with the boy's mother, who yelled at him for not telling her about it immediately. She then reported the incident to law enforcement officials. During the subsequent investigation, Oei mentioned the image on his phone, and he was charged with possessing child pornography. It cost him $150,000 to defend himself. Finally, roughly a year after Oei's troubles began, a Virginia judge dismissed the charges against him on the grounds that the sexted image did not qualify as pornography because the girl's breasts were not exposed and her pose was not sexually suggestive.

that the girl might not have seen it that way. Instead, she could have been traumatized by unexpectedly receiving a photo of the boy's genitals, in which case this event could be seen as a type of bullying. Therefore, critics of the study suggest, the boy's sexting was serious enough to have been included in the researchers' statistics.

Depression

Studies have shown that teens who are bullied via sexting are very likely to be depressed. A study released in November 2011 by the Education Development Center in Massachusetts connects sexting to other psychological problems as well, including suicidal thoughts. Researchers do not know whether sexting actually causes depression and increases suicide risk, or whether people who feel bad about themselves are simply more drawn to sexting. But either way, their finding that 13 percent of teens involved in sexting have tried to commit suicide, as compared to 3 percent of teens who do not sext, is a matter of concern.

Cases like Hope Witsell's also illustrate this point. But in her case and a similar notable case from 2008, that of eighteen-year-old Jessica Logan of Cincinnati, Ohio, the trigger for the suicide was the bullying associated with the sexting. Jessica sexted nude photos of herself to her boyfriend, and after they broke up he forwarded the pictures to other people without her permission. Jessica then became the target of sexual harassment at her high school, and the harassment grew worse after she talked about the issue of sexting on a television news program. During graduation festivities, classmates threw drinks on her and forced her from parties; shortly after graduation, Jessica hanged herself in her bedroom. Her parents subsequently sued the school for not protecting their daughter from harassment, and her story gained widespread media attention as the first publicized case of sexting-associated suicide.

No Big Deal

Despite such cases, however, many teens do not see sexting as a serious problem. In fact, some see it as no problem at all. For example, one seventeen-year-old from Maryland reports, "If a boy meets a girl or has a girlfriend on summer break he comes back and shows all his boys the [naked] pictures he's been sent. No one gives it that much thought really."[76]

Similarly, columnist Jeff A. Katz of the *Cornell Daily Sun* college newspaper reports that on his campus it is not unusual for guys to share sexts. During one conversation, he says, "It took all but three seconds for the group of guys I asked about sexting to start talking to me about the pictures they'd received." He also tells about a friend whose phone accidentally recorded a voicemail of the friend having sex. Katz says, "Guess how I know about it. Yeah, I heard that message."[77]

Experts say that with boys, this type of sharing is often a way to brag. And in doing so, many boys cannot conceive that what they are doing or saying might hurt the girl who sexted the photo. In part this is because teens have trouble seeing that something that seems fun at the moment might actually cause harm later. Victor Strasburger, a specialist in adolescent medicine at the University of New Mexico, explains that this trouble stems from the fact that the teenage brain has not yet developed the ability to recognize the consequences of actions like sexting. He says "teenagers are neurologically programmed to do dumb things."[78]

With girls, more often the issue is that they view sexting as acceptable because the celebrities they idolize have sexted or allowed nude pictures of themselves to be distributed via other means. As a result of celebrity behavior, according to Joe Kelly, president of the website Dads and Daughters, "young people . . . are starting to think that it's normal to show flesh in social settings, particularly through technology."[79] Moreover, girls wanting to be as popular as a reality TV star, for example, can decide to sext a picture as a way to gain celebrity among peers. Laurie Ouellete of the University of Minnesota, an expert on reality TV, says, "The price [of becoming famous] is that you have to define yourself in the same kind of terms that celebrities are defined."[80]

The prevalence of nudity in popular culture has another effect—that of desensitizing people to the point that nudity is no longer shocking. The same is true for sexually suggestive or graphic images shown on television or in movies. With the spread of cable channels that do not censor such images, more young people are being exposed to scenes they would not have been allowed to see years ago. This is the case, for example, with teen fans of the popular HBO TV series *Game of Thrones*, a richly told fantasy story with kid-appealing elements like knights and dragons that also contains graphic violence and sex.

Boyfriend Revenge

Even teens who are not bothered by on-screen nudity can feel uncomfortable with the idea of sexting nude pictures of themselves—and yet some do it anyway. Surveys have found that older teenage girls who sext often do so in order to keep their boyfriends sexually satisfied in a way that does not involve actual sex, accepting the discomfort of taking and sharing nude photos of themselves in order to avoid the discomfort of being pressured to have sex. A partner's demand for such photos is generally considered a form of abuse. But regardless of whether the sexting was the result of coercion, surveys show that most sexts are sent to a romantic interest. According to one survey by the National Campaign to Prevent Teen and Unplanned Pregnancy and *CosmoGirl.com*, over 70 percent of girls who have sexted say their nude or semi-nude images were intended for a boyfriend, and only slightly fewer than 70 percent of boys who have sexted say their images were for girlfriends.

But what many teens conveniently forget is that images sent to a boyfriend or girlfriend can be saved and kept—and if the couple breaks up, the partner who supplied the nude pictures can be in for an unpleasant surprise. The media has reported on several cases in recent years involving an ex-boyfriend exacting revenge on his former girlfriend by sharing photos she sexted to him when they were together. Consequently the website LoveIsRespect.org says,

> Does your partner ask for inappropriate pictures of you? Or send them to you? Even if you trust that your partner will be the only one to ever see the pictures, you can never guarantee that they won't end up on someone else's phone or online. Seriously consider playing it safe and making a policy of not sending and instantly deleting inappropriate photos. The same goes for webcams and instant messaging, too. Remember you never have to do anything you aren't comfortable with, no matter how much your partner pressures you.[81]

Legal Troubles

Regardless of how sexts come to exist or who disseminates them, they can have serious consequences for teens because most adults

"Even if you trust that your partner will be the only one to ever see the pictures, you can never guarantee that they won't end up on someone else's phone or online."[81]

— LoveIsRespect.org.

The fantasy television series Game of Thrones, *based on the books by George R.R. Martin, features knights and dragons as well as graphic sex and violence. This and other pop culture offerings may have a desensitizing effect on teen viewers. Actress Emilia Clarke, who plays Daenerys Targaryen, appears here in a scene from the television series.*

do not view them as funny or innocent or harmless. Instead, officials typically punish a teen who appears in a sexually suggestive photo or video. This was the case with Hope Witsell's suspension. Another example is a 2009 case in which high school girls were kicked off their cheerleading squad for having taken nude photos of themselves. These cheerleaders did not send the photos to classmates, but an unknown culprit did, and those classmates then for-

Blocking Sexts

In October 2010 Apple was granted a patent on technology that would allow parents to block other people from sending their teens sexually explicit messages. Still in development, the cell phone application, or app, would filter out certain sexually charged words, and as envisioned the app would also be able to use standard vocabulary from the child's own grade level to determine what words to filter. Parents could also create a list of words for the filter to recognize and block. Conversely, parents could create a list of words that their child had to use over a certain period of time, thereby turning texting into a learning tool. In press releases on the new technology, an example of this usage was a teen studying a foreign language being required to text at least part of the time in that language. What the filter would not be able to do, however, is block the sending or receiving of any kind of photo or video, including sexually explicit ones. Nonetheless, when news of this app broke, the media dubbed it "the sext blocker."

warded them to other classmates and the school principal. Those who forwarded the images were never punished.

Other cases involve far more serious consequences—legal ones, because in many places the law considers sexting to be a form of pornography. If the images depict a minor (most often defined as someone under the age of eighteen), then it is considered child pornography, and someone who possesses such an image can be prosecuted as a child pornographer. If that person is a legal adult, once convicted the individual can be required to register as a sex offender.

This happened to Phillip Alpert of Florida, who was eighteen at the time he was charged. His sexting-related legal troubles began after he woke up one morning angry about a fight with his sixteen-year-old girlfriend and decided to send a few naked pictures of her to more than seventy people. Then he went back to sleep. In a 2010 interview on the TV show *ABC Nightline*, Alpert said that after he sexted the pictures, "I forgot I did it. I was barely awake when I did it and I didn't even remember and . . . then a few days later, my mother called and says, 'Why are there police officers at the house?' I went—'Oh no!' And it came back the same way a dream does."[82]

Unfair Punishment

Alpert subsequently pled guilty to possessing and distributing child pornography, and as a result of his criminal proceedings, he must remain on a national list of child sex offenders until he is forty-three years old. This means he cannot live near schools or linger in places where large numbers of children are known to gather, such as playgrounds and beaches. In addition, his history will make it more difficult for him to get a job. He feels all of this is unfair, although he also feels great remorse over hurting the girl whose photos he sexted. He says that he wants to tell her, "I am sorry. I really am, and it's not because I'm a sex offender, because I got kicked out of school, because I'm on probation, I can't go to the beach, whatever. It's because what I did and I'm sorry for it. And I mean, I said it. I can't do anything else besides say I'm sorry over and over and over, and I don't think it's enough, but it's all I've got right now."[83]

Alpert's attorney, Lawrence Walters, believes that his client's punishment is ridiculous, although he acknowledges that what Alpert did was wrong. He says, "Phillip did something that about 20 or 30 percent of high school students do, and it is a mistake, it is something that shouldn't be done, nobody condones. On the other hand, we have a legal system that treats this behavior as something horrendous, on par with child molestation—and it simply isn't. . . . The law simply hasn't recognized this unique phenomenon of children texting, or sexting each other, in high school."[84]

New York Times columnist Emily Bazelon agrees. In an editorial she complains,

> "A conviction for child pornography can trigger heavy punishment . . . that's too harsh for teenagers in all but the most egregious cases."[85]
>
> — *New York Times* columnist Emily Bazelon.

In the panic over teenager sexting, some prosecutors are going too far, turning the child-pornography laws that are supposed to protect children into a weapon that can be used against them. The easiest way to crack down on teenagers who send around sexual photos is to charge them as if they're child pornographers. But . . . a conviction for child pornography can trigger heavy punishment . . . that's too harsh for teenagers in all but the most egregious cases.[85]

Changes in Law

Also agreeing with this position is New York University (NYU) law professor Amy Adler, who says, "Technically, it is child pornography. But I don't think it's the kind of case where child pornography law is the right legal framework to use to judge it."[86] Adler points out that child pornography laws were designed to keep pedophiles from preying on children and argues that they should not apply to cases involving teen couples like Alpert and his girlfriend. Instead, Adler suggests, situations like theirs should be addressed with laws that apply to cases in which someone's privacy has been invaded.

Indeed, a few states have changed their laws to reflect the idea that an image sexted from one teen to another should be judged differently than the kind of child pornography that adult sexual predators disseminate. Other states are considering changing existing laws or drafting new ones to ensure that teens are not punished too harshly for sexting. For example, in March 2011 North Dakota passed a law that would allow authorities to use their discretion in prosecuting cases of sexting by charging only individuals who intended to humiliate or otherwise emotionally harm someone by sexting.

> "You should delete [a sext as soon as you receive one] and not tell anybody. If it doesn't get disseminated and distributed, it's ended."[87]
>
> — Justin Patchin, codirector of the Cyberbullying Research Center.

Delete It and Forget It

Until more states address this issue, however, some people recommend that young people avoid bringing a sexted image to the attention of authorities. For example, Justin Patchin, codirector of the Cyberbullying Research Center, tells teens who have received a sext: "You should delete it and not tell anybody. If it doesn't get disseminated and distributed, it's ended. . . . If you tell adults, you're throwing that person [who sent you the sext] under the bus."[87]

In defense of this position, Patchin adds, "Adults, it seems, are forced to respond to sexting in extreme ways—ways that have long-term, irreversible consequences. Until we can develop reasonable responses that do not potentially foreclose on the futures of all involved, we are wise to advise that students do not contact adults, unless the situation is appearing to get out of control. And I think teens know when it is out of control."[88]

Other experts believe it is irresponsible to tell young people not to report sexually charged situations to authorities, because this might also lead children and teens to fail to report truly serious cases of sexual predation. According to law enforcement authorities, sexual predation via cell phone is on the rise, and young people need to be aware that the risks associated with responding to the texts of a stranger or near stranger, especially texts of a sexual nature, are just as serious as responding to similar messages on the Internet. And as with online predation, sometimes a person reaching out via text is pretending to be someone else—a classmate or peer, for example—or the predator is an adult friend, relative, teacher, or other authority figure who uses texts and calls to gradually encourage a sexual relationship with the teen, escalating the cell phone exchanges from flirting to sexting to face-to-face sexual encounters.

"The whole issue of the nude photograph being distributed through cell phones, we're still looking at."[89]

— J.D. Callaway, a spokesperson for the Hillsborough County Sheriff's Office.

Nonetheless, authorities do acknowledge that the criminal justice system is not addressing the problem of sexting adequately. This is evident from the fact that teenage boys and girls continue to be arrested for sexting pictures to one another. Consequently J.D. Callaway, a spokesperson for the Hillsborough County Sheriff's Office involved in the Hope Witsell case, says, "The whole issue of the nude photograph being distributed through cell phones, we're still looking at."[89]

Facts

- In an AP/MTV poll of teens who have forwarded a sexted photo or video to others, the top reasons for forwarding the image were because it seemed funny, because they thought everybody would want to see the image, and because they were bored.

- Surveys show that most teens who sext do it more than once.

- According to the Pew Internet & American Life Project, one-third of college students sext.

- Both males and females admit to sexting pictures of themselves, although females are slightly more likely to do so than males. Conversely, males are slightly more likely than females to receive sexts from others.

- Studies suggest that nearly one-fifth of teens who receive a sext then pass it along to at least one other person.

Source Notes

Introduction: Heavy Usage

1. Quoted in Erik Runge, "Friends: Teen Driver Killed in Crash Was Texting, Not Wearing Seat Belt," March 26, 2012. www.myfoxtwincities .com.

2. Amanda Lenhart et al., *Teens and Mobile Phones*, Pew Internet & American Life Project, Pew Research Center, April 20, 2010. http://pewinternet .org.

3. jnazeri12, "Teens Too Reliant over Technology," Teen Ink. www.teenink .com.

4. David Crystal, *Txtng: The Gr8 Db8*. New York: Oxford University, 2009, p. 170.

5. Quoted in Crystal, *Txtng: The Gr8 Db8*, p. 171.

6. Crystal, *Txtng: The Gr8 Db8*, p. 173.

Chapter One: What Are the Origins of the Teen Cell Phone Use Controversy?

7. Sarah Gilbert, "Avoiding Cell Bill Meltdown with Your Teen or Tween," Five Cent Nickel. www.fivecentnickel.com.

8. Quoted in Margaret Webb Pressler, "For Texting Teens, an OMG Moment When the Phone Bill Arrives," *Washington Post*, May 20, 2007. www.washingtonpost.com.

9. Quoted in Adam Chodak, "Dad Hammers Wyoming Teen's Phone After Mega-Bill," *Denver Post*, April 8, 2009. www.denverpost.com.

10. Quoted in JP Mangalindan, "Teen Racks Up $21,917 Cell Phone Bill, Dad Flabbergasted," HuffPost Tech, December 14, 2009. www.switched .com.

11. Quoted in Katie Hafner, "Texting May Be Taking a Toll," *New York Times*, May 26, 2009. www.nytimes.com.

12. Quoted in Pressler, "For Texting Teens, an OMG Moment When the Phone Bill Arrives."

13. Shawn Marie Edgington, *The Parent's Guide to Texting, Facebook, and Social Media*. Dallas: Brown, 2011, p. 38.

14. Quoted in Chodak, "Dad Hammers Wyoming Teen's Phone After Mega-Bill."

15. Russell A. Sabella, "Cell Phones, Texting and Cell Phone Distractions," Education.com. www.education.com.

16. Frederick S. Lane, *Cybertraps for the Young*. Chicago: NTI Upstream, 2011, p. 14.

17. Lane, *Cybertraps for the Young*, p. 14.

18. Quoted in Nate Stewart, "Cyber Predators Targeting Cell Phones," wltx .com, March 3, 2011. www.wltx.com.

19. Edgington, *The Parent's Guide to Texting, Facebook, and Social Media*, pp. 34–35.

20. Richard Guerry, *Public and Permanent: The Golden Rule of the 21st Century*. Bloomington, IN: Balboa, 2011, p. 61.

21. Quoted in Danielle Dellorto, "WHO: Cell Phone Use Can Increase Possible Cancer Risk," CNN, May 31, 2011. www.cnn.com.

22. Quoted in Dan Levine, "Cell Phone Study Raises Profile on Safety Lawsuits," Reuters, June 1, 2011. www.reuters.com.

Chapter Two: How Do Cell Phones Impact Personal Relationships?

23. Cathy J. Wilson, "Texting Provides Dangerous Outlet for Dating Violence," June 22, 2010. http://open.salon.com.

24. Wilson, "Texting Provides Dangerous Outlet for Dating Violence."

25. Quoted in Donna St. George, "Text Messages Become a Growing Weapon in Dating Violence," *Washington Post*, June 21, 2010. www.washing tonpost.com.

26. Quoted in St. George, "Text Messages Become a Growing Weapon in Dating Violence."

27. Amar Toor, "Text Messages Become Catalysts for Dating Violence," Huff-Post Tech, June 22, 2010. www.switched.com.

28. Quoted in St. George, "Text Messages Become a Growing Weapon in Dating Violence."

29. Quoted in Elizabeth Olson, "A Rise in Efforts to Spot Abuse in Youth Dating," Time's Up!, February 2010. http://timesupblog.blogspot.com.

30. Quoted in Olson, "A Rise in Efforts to Spot Abuse in Youth Dating."

31. Quoted in Lenhart et al., *Teens and Mobile Phones*.

32. Jenna Welsh, "Teen Scene: How Much Texting Is Too Much?," *Gettysburg Times*, August 17, 2010. www.gettysburgtimes.com.

33. Quoted in Crystal, *Txtng: The Gr8 Db8*, p. 29.

34. Guerry, *Public and Permanent*, p. 25.

35. Lane, *Cybertraps for the Young*, p. 91.

36. Lane, *Cybertraps for the Young*, p. 91.

37. Crystal, *Txtng: The Gr8 Db8*, p. 171.

38. Quoted in Crystal, *Txtng: The Gr8 Db8*, p. 171.

39. Christopher McCarthy, "The Benefits of Texting & Facebook for Teens and Reasons Why Parents Should Allow It Within Limits," November 13, 2010. http://blog.myanxiouschild.com.

40. McCarthy, "The Benefits of Texting & Facebook for Teens."

41. Martha Filipic, "Cell Phones and Parent-Teen Relationships," 2011. http://fayette.osu.edu.

42. Quoted in American University, "Being Always On Impacts Personal Relationships More than It Impacts the Written Language," *Science Daily*, May 20, 2008. www.sciencedaily.com.

43. Quoted in American University, "Being Always On Impacts Personal Relationships More than It Impacts the Written Language."

44. Karen Gail Lewis, "Cell Phones and Relationships." www.drkarengaillewis.com.

Chapter Three: Is Cell Phone Addiction a Problem?

45. Jerry Tillotson, "Teenage Cell Phone Addiction," HubPages, January 2, 2010. http://jerrytillotson.hubpages.com.

46. Tillotson, "Teenage Cell Phone Addiction."

47. Lewis, "Cell Phones and Relationships."

48. Quoted in KPLR 11 News of St. Louis, Missouri, "'Nomophobia'—Cell Phone Addiction on the Rise," March 7, 2012. http://kplr11.com.

49. Quoted in KPLR 11 News of St. Louis, Missouri, "'Nomophobia'—Cell Phone Addiction on the Rise."

50. Quoted in Stephanie Guzman, "Local CHP Officers Taking Aim at Distracted Drivers This Month," *Simi Valley Acorn*, April 20, 2012, p. 8.

51. Cellphone Addiction, "Cell Phone Addiction and Texting Addiction," November 5, 2011. http://cellphoneaddiction.org.

52. Quoted in *Huffington Post*, "Smartphones and Posture: Are Your Phone Habits Killing Your Neck and Back?," January 19, 2012. www.huffingtonpost.com.

53. Quoted in Bill Hendrick, "Texting Can Be a Pain in the Neck, Shoulders," Web MD, November 12, 2009. www.webmd.com.

54. Quoted in Majid Siddique, "Computer Games, Texting Raise Long-Term Musculoskeletal Pain in Kids," AAJ News, April 30, 2012. www.aaj.tv.

55. Quoted in National Sleep Foundation, "Annual Sleep in America Poll Exploring Connections with Communications Technology Use and Sleep," press release, March 7, 2011. www.sleepfoundation.org.

56. Quoted in Sharon Gaudin, "Can't Sleep? Blame Your Computer, Cell Phone," *Computerworld*, March 7, 2011. www.computerworld.com.

57. Quoted in National Sleep Foundation, "Annual Sleep in America Poll Exploring Connections with Communications Technology Use and Sleep."

Chapter Four: How Serious a Problem Is Cell Phone Use While Driving?

58. Quoted in *PBS NewsHour*, "Cell Phone Use Raises Risks While Driving, Studies Show," transcript, PBS, July 28, 2009. www.pbs.org.

59. David L. Strayer and Frank A. Drews, "Cell-Phone-Induced Driver Distraction," *Current Directions in Psychological Science*, vol. 16, no. 3, 2007, p. 128.

60. Quoted in *PBS NewsHour*, "Cell Phone Use Raises Risks While Driving, Studies Show."

61. Quoted in Jim Forsyth, "Texting While Driving More Dangerous than Thought," Reuters, October 5, 2011. www.reuters.com.

62. Michael Austin, "Texting While Driving: How Dangerous Is It?," *Car and Driver*, June 2009. www.caranddriver.com.

63. Austin, "Texting While Driving: How Dangerous Is It?"

64. Phil LeBeau, "Texting and Driving Worse than Drinking and Driving," CNBC, June 25, 2009. www.cnbc.com.

65. Strayer and Drews, "Cell-Phone-Induced Driver Distraction," p. 129.

66. LeBeau, "Texting and Driving Worse than Drinking and Driving."

67. Austin, "Texting While Driving: How Dangerous Is It?"

68. Quoted in Jim Forsyth, "U.S. Ban Sought on Cell Phone Use While Driving," Reuters, April 26, 2012. www.reuters.com.

69. Quoted in Peter Roff, "Don't Ban Driving with Cell Phones," *U.S. News & World Report*, April 27, 2012. www.usnews.com.

70. Quoted in Mannix Porterfield, "New Texting, Cellular Phone Law Welcomed by Insurers," *Register-Herald* (Beckley, WV), May 7, 2012. www.register-herald.com.

71. Quoted in Porterfield, "New Texting, Cellular Phone Law Welcomed by Insurers."

72. Quoted in Collette Bender, "Cell Phone Ban Not Deterring Nevada Drivers," *Guardian Express* (Las Vegas, NV), May 2012. http://guardianlv.com.

73. Fox5Vegas, "Jane," comments section. www.fox5vegas.com.

74. Quoted in Guzman, "Local CHP Officers Taking Aim at Distracted Drivers This Month."

Chapter Five: How Serious a Problem Is Sexting?

75. Quoted in Lindsey Tanner, "Study: Kids Under 18 Send Few 'Sexting' Messages," KATU TV, December 5, 2011. www.katu.com.

76. Quoted in Gigi Stone, ABC News, "'Sexting' Teens Can Go Too Far," December 14, 2008. www.thenationalcampaign.org.

77. Jeff A. Katz, "Warning: The Dangers of Sexting," *Huffington Post*, February 5, 2012. www.huffingtonpost.com.

78. Quoted in Tanner, "Study: Kids Under 18 Send Few 'Sexting' Messages."

79. Quoted in Chris Wagner, "The Latest Cell Phone Use: Sexting," Center for Parent-Youth Understanding, 2008. www.cpyu.org.

80. Quoted in Wagner, "The Latest Cell Phone Use: Sexting."

81. LoveIsRespect.org, "Texting and Sexting." www.loveisrespect.org.

82. Quoted in Vicki Mabrey and David Perozzi, "Sexting: Should Child Pornography Laws Apply?," transcript, *ABC Nightline*, April 1, 2010, p. 1. http://abcnews.go.com.

83. Quoted in Mabrey and Perozzi, "Sexting: Should Child Pornography Laws Apply?," p. 3.

84. Quoted in Mabrey and Perozzi, "Sexting: Should Child Pornography Laws Apply?," p. 2.

85. Emily Bazelon, "The Ninny State," *New York Times*, June 24, 2011. www.nytimes.com.

86. Quoted in Mabrey and Perozzi, "Sexting: Should Child Pornography Laws Apply?," p. 1.

87. Quoted in Lisa Esposito, "Teen 'Sexting' Common and Linked to Psychological Woes," Fox 12 Oregon, November 3, 2011. www.kptv.com.

88. Quoted in Esposito, "Teen 'Sexting' Common and Linked to Psychological Woes."

89. Quoted in Andrew Meacham, "Sexting-Related Bullying Cited in Hillsborough Teen's Suicide," *Tampa Bay Times*, November 29, 2009. www.tampabay.com.

Related Organizations and Websites

Cell Phone Safety

website: www.cellphonesafety.org

Created by the National Consumer Advocacy Commission, which works to educate consumers on safety and economic issues surrounding certain products and services, CellPhoneSafety.org concentrates on issues related to the safety and financial concerns related to cell phone use.

CTIA—The Wireless Association

1400 Sixteenth St. NW, Suite 600
Washington, DC 20036
phone: (202) 736-3200
fax: (202) 785-0721

Founded in 1984, this international nonprofit membership organization supports the wireless communications industry and provides information on cell phone–related issues and laws.

Cyberbullying Research Center

website: www.cyberbullying.us

The Cyberbullying Research Center provides up-to-date information about the nature, extent, causes, and consequences of cyberbullying among teens.

Don't Drive and Text
222 N. Main St., Suite A
Bryan, TX 77803
website: http://dontdriveandtext.org

This organization provides information on the dangers of texting and driving as part of a campaign to stop the practice.

Family Online Safety Institute (FOSI)
400 Seventh St. NW, Suite 306
Washington, DC 20004
website: www.fosi.org

An international nonprofit organization, FOSI partners with major communications- and entertainment-related companies to develop a safer Internet while still respecting free speech. It also works with Internet safety advocates and others to develop new technology, shape public policy, and promote education related to online safety.

iKeepSafe
4301 N. Fairfax Dr., Suite 190
Arlington, VA 22203
phone: (703) 717-9066; toll free: (866) 794-7233
fax: (703) 852-7100 Attn: iKeepSafe
e-mail: info@ikeepsafe.org
website: www.ikeepsafe.org

Established in 2005, this group is a nonprofit international alliance of more than one hundred policy leaders, educators, law enforcement members, technology experts, public health experts and advocates dedicated to keeping kids safe in a digital world.

Kids Health
website: http://kidshealth.org

This group provides information for parents, educators, and teens on a variety of health-related issues, including addiction. The TeensHealth section of the website provides a place for teens to receive confidential, accurate information and advice twenty-four hours a day about issues related to health, emotions, and daily life.

Pew Research Center

1615 L St. NW, Suite 700
Washington, DC 20036
phone: (202) 419-4300
fax: (202) 419-4349
website: info@pewresearch.org

The Pew Research Center is a nonpartisan research organization that conducts and analyzes the results of public opinion polls and demographic studies on a variety of issues, attitudes, and trends. Its Pew Internet & American Life Project specifically addresses the impact of the Internet on American life and society and has conducted studies related to cell phone use.

Teen Angels

website: http://teenangels.org

A division of WiredSafety, Teen Angels is a group comprising volunteers ages thirteen to eighteen who have been trained in online safety, privacy, and security and seek to educate others on the dangers associated with going online, whether via a computer or a cell phone.

Text Free Driving Organization

website: www.textfreedriving.org

Based in Florida, this group is dedicated to raising awareness of the dangers of texting and working to support laws that would eliminate cell phone use while driving.

WiredSafety

website: www.wiredsafety.org

Founded in 1995, the nonprofit group WiredSafety helps victims of cybercrime and online harassment, assists law enforcement worldwide in preventing and investigating cybercrimes, and disseminates information designed to educate people on privacy, security, and other aspects of online safety, including those related to cell phone use to access the Internet.

World Health Organization (WHO)

website: www.who.int
Avenue Appia 20
1211 Geneva 27, Switzerland
phone: 41 22 791 21 11
fax: 41 22 791 31 11

WHO supports research into and provides information on a wide variety of health issues, including those related to cell phone use.

Additional Reading

Books

Mark Bauerlein, *The Digital Divide: Arguments for and Against Facebook, Google, Texting, and the Age of Social Networking.* New York: Tarcher, 2011.

Brian X. Chen, *Always On: How the iPhone Unlocked the Anything-Anytime-Anywhere Future—and Locked Us In.* Cambridge, MA: Da Capo, 2011.

Devra Davis, *Disconnect: The Truth About Cell Phone Radiation, What the Industry Has Done to Hide It, and How to Protect Your Family.* New York: Dutton, 2010.

Ann Louise Gittleman, *Zapped: Why Your Cell Phone Shouldn't Be Your Alarm Clock and 1268 Ways to Outsmart the Hazards of Electronic Pollution.* New York: HarperCollins, 2011.

Richard Guerry, *Public and Permanent: The Golden Rule of the 21st Century.* Bloomington, IN: Balboa, 2011.

Frederick S. Lane, *Cybertraps for the Young.* Chicago: NTI Upstream, 2011.

Internet Sources

Nancy V. Gifford, *Sexting in the U.S.A.*, Family Online Safety Institute. www.fosi.org/images/stories/resources/sexting.pdf.

Jennifer A. Hanley, *Cyberbullying: A Global Concern*, Family Online Safety Institute. www.fosi.org/images/stories/resources/cyberbullying.pdf.

Amanda Lenhart et al., *Teens and Mobile Phones*, Pew Internet & American Life Project, Pew Research Center, April 20, 2010. http://pewinternet.org/Reports/2010/Teens-and-Mobile-Pho nes/Summary-of-findings.aspx.

Mary Madden, "Teens, Social Network Sites & Mobile Phones: What the Research Is Telling Us," online slideshow, Pew Internet & American Life Project, Pew Research Center, December 5, 2011. http://www.slideshare.net/mobile/PewInternet/ teens-social-network-sites-mobile-phones-what-the-research -is-telling-us-cosn.

National Campaign to Prevent Teen and Unplanned Pregnancy and *CosmoGirl*.com, *Sex and Tech: Results from a Survey of Teens and Young Adults*. www.thenationalcampaign.org/sex tech/pdf/sextech_summary.pdf.

David L. Strayer and Frank A. Drews, "Cell-Phone-Induced Driver Distraction," *Current Directions in Psychological Science*, vol. 16, no. 3, 2007. www.psych.utah.edu/lab/appliedcognition/ publications/cellphone.pdf.

Index

Note: Boldface page numbers indicate illustrations.

Picture Credits

About the Author

Patricia D. Netzley has written dozens of books for children, teens, and adults. She has also worked as an editor and a writing instructor. She is a member of the Society of Children's Book Writers and Illustrators (SCBWI) and the Romance Writers of America (RWA).